thedogman

Martin McKenna

thedogman

an expert explains dog sense

Martin McKenna

ABC
BOOKS

I'd like to give special thanks to Angela Catterns, Barbara Hagan, Trent O'Keefe and Fiona Wylie from the ABC. But most of all to Leanne and the kids, Siggy, Casey and Fintan.

Published by ABC Books for the
AUSTRALIAN BROADCASTING CORPORATION
GPO Box 9994 Sydney NSW 2001

Copyright © Martin McKenna 2001

First published 2001

National Library of Australia
Cataloguing-in-Publication entry
McKenna, Martin Anthony.
  The Dogman: an expert explains dog sense.

  ISBN 0 7333 0904 6

  1. Dogs - Psychology - Handbooks, manuals, etc. 2. Dogs - Training -
  Handbooks, manuals, etc. 3. Dogs - Behaviour - Handbooks, manuals,
  etc. I. Australian Broadcasting Corporation. II. Title

636.70835

Designed and typeset by Kerry Klinner
Photography by Gary Johnston
Set in Sabon 10/14 pt
Printed and bound in Australia by Griffin Press Pty. Ltd.

5 4 3 2 1

contents

foreword

When you sit down with Martin McKenna like I have and he tells you his story, ending it with a definite, "And that's when I knew I was a dog, eh?", you can't be blamed for thinking, "And you're an absolute loony, eh?" But spend more time with him, like I have, to feel his passion, ponder his wisdom and share his warmth, and you realise you're onto something special. It's not just a cute bit of Irish blarney — although Martin's got a personal sparkle and a turn of phrase that turns the blood to Guinness. Nor is it entirely a by-product of his disillusionment with humankind after his bleak and bitter childhood in Ireland, although you couldn't blame him if it were! It'd also be wrong to blame it too much on the overwhelming Attention Deficit Disorder (coloured by a big dose of hyperactivity) which has further complicated his life. It's none of these things, and all of them.

Martin's story is as great as it is unusual. One of the greatest things about it is that today, on his little piece of Australia hacked off the front corner of an old banana farm on the far north coast of New South Wales, where he lives in characteristic chaos with Leanne and their trio of cheekily grinning ankle-biters, Martin doesn't dwell much on the trials, troubles and turmoils of his past. He's at peace with his fellow man. He'd be even more so if we were prepared to live in peace with his fellow dogs.

Martin sees the world through the eyes of the dogs who he feels nurtured and inspired him when things were at their worst. You may have heard him on ABC Radio, dispensing his earthy, no bullshit, simple commonsense advice to Australian dog owners. You may even be one of the scores of people who've rung him, seeking personal guidance on how to deal with a troublesome pooch. If you've heard him or spoken to him, I bet you've said to yourself, "Of course. Why didn't I think of that?"

As you'll know, Martin loves a chat and sometimes it's easy to forget whose side he's really on. It should come as no surprise that because he sees our world from a dog's point of view, Martin McKenna's advice often flies in the face of conventional dog care wisdom. He doesn't see dogs as people — he expresses our world in their terms. As he says himself, "It's totally against what all those professors and people say, eh?"

But he does so safe in the knowledge that, as a dog, he knows a sight more than they ever could, eh? To quote him, "This book in its simplicity is going to inadvertently help the human. Because dogs are so simple and because they don't need the complexity of big theories, it's going to make it simple for everyone. That's the key word. This is a simple book about simple creatures."

Where do I fit in all of this? Well, as Martin sees himself as a translator on behalf of all dogs, I'm his translator. While Martin McKenna is without a doubt one of the most intelligent, eloquent and persuasive blokes I've ever met, that old ADD has robbed him of the ability to put it down as words on a page. So I've crossed the T's and dotted the I's for him. That's all I've done here. And I've listened and learned. I've found out that everything I do with my dogs is almost 100 per cent wrong. After years of living, working and writing about them, I find I know sweet bugger-all.

Everything you read from now on is pure Martin McKenna. After hours spent in his living room or in a motel with my little tape-recorder rattling away and Martin expounding his passion and commitment, I can only hope I've managed to capture it well enough to pass on to everyone else.

I've tried to preserve the real essence of Martin. Oh, sure, I've deleted the odd expletive. But not all of them. So the odd turn of phrase may catch some readers off guard. Those of you won over by the staid old British "Walkies!" school of nice, conservative, middle-class, middle-aged dog communication may be horribly offended. But, as Martin will tell you, this is the dog world we're entering. It's also his world. The funny thing is though, if you stick with us you'll undoubtedly regain any faith you may have lost in the human spirit. You'll also learn a lot about what it's like to be a dog, and what you should be doing to make the old proverbial dog's life a little more like we perceive it to be.

But don't feel too smug at the end of it. Don't forget that Martin's not doing this for you. He's doing it for the dogs. He's the Dogman, eh?

Mike Hayes
"Prickle Farm"
January 2001

part 1

the dogman

chapter 1

my puppy days

People call me the Dogman because I have an uncanny knack of being able to tell people why their dog is doing what it's doing. In a funny kind of way I've been able to teach them how to talk back to their dog — by understanding a few signals and a few little messages that they need to remember in their everyday doings with their dog.

I first started doing that when I was a kid, living on the streets of Limerick, in Ireland. Why did I live like that? To be quite truthful, I was too bold and nasty for family life, eh?

To take that truth even further — the full story isn't a pretty one. In fact, the first time we got it all down, it seemed pretty bitter and twisted, which wasn't what I intended at all. I don't want my life to be some sob story like *Angela's Ashes*. I only want to mention the hardship I suffered when I was a young feller to show how anyone can win out through just about anything if they're willing to find the strength to overcome it.

That strength stays with you forever.

And I found it through dogs — through being able to relate to them. I received so much inspiration from them that I reckon I owe them something back. So whatever happened to me I'm not unhappy about any more, so long as my story can help other people relate to dogs.

I think I came to the conclusion that I preferred being a dog to being a human about the time I was first able to think. Limerick in the 1960s was poor. You couldn't call us working class, because there was nobody working. There was just an underclass of people struggling to make it in a country that hadn't had an Industrial Revolution.

The pubs in Garryowen where we lived were good — too good. That was the problem. The husbands always spent their time in the pubs instead of being at home with their family. The pub was next door to the church. When you went to church, the priest would say, "Make sure you give that wife of yours a flogging … and them kids a flogging … to keep them in line." The ordinary men would all stand at the back of the church. Just after the sermon started, they'd all nick out to the pub.

My father was no different to any of them. I'll be fair to him. When he was good he was very good. But by Christ when he was bad … He was a brilliant man. He could have run any major company. This man was six foot seven, and he looked like Cary Grant with the black wavy hair. People admired him and used to follow him round in the street. They must have known a different father to me. Because when he came home he was totally different.

My father wasn't a bad man. He was really funny when he wanted to be. I think that's one of the reasons my mother loved him. He certainly gave me my humour. It might seem a contradiction in terms but the humour that he had, I used to learn to laugh at my own circumstances.

But the drink got in the way. People used to tell him, "Mick, you could pull your whole family out of the shit." But he just wasn't strong enough to do it. We had good times, but the stress of having our kind of a family was too dynamic. There were too many opposing forces involved.

Why was he the way he was? Who really knows? Maybe it had something to do with the shock of deciding to come back to Ireland at a time when there was no work and everyone else was trying to leave, with a beautiful German wife who hardly spoke English at first, and then having Andrew, John and me — triplets.

The handsomest little dudes you'd ever see in a lifetime — the McKenna triplets.

And who knows? He could have had what my brothers and I had. What we had was later diagnosed as what we now call Attention Deficit Disorder, topped up with severe hyperactivity.

When we were born, we created quite a stir. We were identical triplets — the handsomest little dudes you'd ever see in a lifetime: blond hair, perfect skins, nice little fellers, beautiful smiles. People came from England, Germany and all over Ireland to photograph us. It must have seemed to everybody in Garryowen like the Second Coming. They must have thought, "These people are going to have a good life, eh?" Not quite.

For a start, when we were born we weighed only two pound, one ounce each. We were very sick. We were incubated for at least six months, so we were rarely ever touched by human beings. That played a great part in the dog I was to become. When you're not handled at that formative stage of your life, when you're not hugged and you're not interacted with, normal human bonding won't happen. That connection won't be made.

But if you put three babies in a cot, they'll talk to each other through their minds. It's pretty much the same with puppies in a den. They'll communicate way before they'll understand what their proper skills are. But no matter how beneficial and positive I can actually regard all that now, at the time no one had any idea.

Our neighbours' attitudes to us certainly didn't help. People become suspicious easily in Ireland. In our case, they put two and fifty-five together — and came up with nine. They decided we were some kind of Hitler's babies and that my Mammy had been part of some experiment in Germany with children. She used to laugh her guts out because she'd spent most of the Second World War running around looking for food, dodging Allied bombs and all that stuff. I don't know where she would have got the time for medical experiments.

My Mammy might have been able to laugh all that off, but she certainly couldn't cope with us. No one could blame her, or the rest of the family, for that matter. Have you any idea what it's like to have ADD triplets bouncing off the walls twenty-four hours a day? It'd drive twenty mothers insane. You couldn't get twenty mothers to look after us. No wonder we were often farmed out, inevitably with disastrous results.

One of the flashbacks I get from our childhood involves various people we stayed with. In this flash I have we were in this house, three if us in the same bed, and there's a picture up on the wall. It was some dude and his heart was bleeding and he's holding this "thing", this light, in his hand. I knew later what it was but I didn't know then. We just kept looking at it.

"What is it?"

No idea.

"Let's kill it!"

So we did. Then we got flogged by the people we were staying with for punching the living daylights out of their religious relic.

There were eight kids in the family. We got singled out all the time. Me, Andrew and John were always segregated. That was another way we learned about being dogs. We were always at the bottom. We were always supervised by someone else in the family. We couldn't do anything on our own. It was like there was them and they were normal, and there was us...

Looking back, our brothers and sisters were probably more traumatised than we were, having to put up with us. They probably paid a lot higher price than we did. Our very strong mother tried to keep it all together. One of the main reasons she couldn't is because the outside world couldn't understand us.

People would stare at us all the time. Being triplets exacerbated it. That probably contributed more to my fear of people than most other things. It's like with a dog. If everyone constantly stares at it and it *knows* it isn't the pack leader, then they *must* be staring a it for another reason ... and that is to attack it.

People wouldn't allow their children to play with us. They totally isolated us. And we weren't the only ones this happened to. There were lots of people worse off than us. There were more families that were good than were bad. The problem was that the good families wouldn't help out the bad. They went the Catholic way of, "Oh no, he's beating his wife but it's not our problem, so we won't worry about it."

Doctors can theorise all they like about ADD but you don't really know it unless you've got it. Your brain craves information. It's like your brain is ahead of your body all the time. It won't shut down. It's like your brain has taken control and it's saying, "I want to know everything and I want to know it *right now*! That's why I can't read too well. Words move around and I get really angry if I can't understand something. My attitude then is, "Forget it!"

A lot of ADD sufferers gravitate to animals. And like animals, they're hypersensitive. With ADD you receive all these emotional messages from people. You're constantly trying to analyse everything and your brain is constantly in overdrive. But what doesn't kill you makes you stronger.

Back in Garryowen, the doctors would say, "We don't know what's wrong with them. Let's give them these tablets, or those ones!"

And then my father would go, "No, let's starve them and flog them and if they don't slow down, throw them out in the coal shed."

That shed was freezing, and we used to sleep in there with the dogs — Major and Rex. They were the loves of our life, and our mother's. She used to wash them in the bath.

Sometimes she'd work as a waitress in a hotel. On a typical day she'd get up about four o'clock, prepare whatever she'd been able to scrounge from the hotel the night before for our breakfast and then be off on her bike in the freezing cold. She'd do two or three jobs and bring food home.

We did our own small bit too, sometimes. Although everyone else disliked us, we could really get on with foreigners. Near where we lived was St Patrick's Well. Not *the* St Patrick's Well, but one of hundreds of them all around Ireland. Ours was pretty neat. It was supposed to be the place where St Patrick's donkey collapsed under him and he had to keep going wherever he was heading on foot. There were probably only twenty or so other places making exactly the same claim. Anyway, when the foreign tourists came they didn't only get the well. They got us. I reckon we were the first tourist marketing board in Ireland.

"Oh my God, Harry, look at the triplets."

We were just an image. They didn't now what we were really like. We'd give them a guided tour. They'd give us dollars. Everyone wanted to photograph the triplets. The dollars helped Mammy with the food.

We'd tell the tourists, "When you go back to America, don't forget to tell people that we're here." How's that for marketing? And it worked. A few months later, other people would turn up.

"You're the triplets. We saw your picture in New York ... or Philadelphia ... or somewhere."

We theorised that if we could relate so easily to foreigners, we must have been foreigners too. Home certainly didn't feel like somewhere we belonged. Because we triplets couldn't communicate with our own family, because we'd never been socialised as babies and because we'd never been socialised with other children before we went to school, starting school was a bloody fiasco.

On our first day, we barricaded ourselves into the classroom and started throwing chairs at the teachers, attacking them like wild animals. Without Mammy we were like dogs tied up, with strangers approaching. We had no retreat, our pack leader was gone. What did they expect us to do? You must remember that we'd been locked in our room most of the time until then.

There's no communication. To all intents and purposes, we're being attacked by aliens. That's what we were like — dogs reacting as though the people coming towards us were attacking our pack. And so we reacted like dogs under attack.

Needless to say, school was a total waste of time. It makes sense. No dog ever benefited from the human education system, eh? I couldn't learn because I was living in a constant state of trauma, starting from the very minute my feet hit the floor in the morning. I still remember the sound of that belt coming off the rack and my old man saying, "If you wet the bed ..."

Jesus! Of *course* I'd wet the damn bed.

Why?

Because I was afraid.

What was I afraid of?

My old man flogging me.

It was a deadly circle. You'd get a flogging first thing in the morning, you'd get no breakfast and you'd be kicked off to school.

You try learning in an environment like that. You're crazy. You can't.

We used to steal everybody's lunch. Again, we had to. We were starving. We used to set it up so we were put outside the classroom for what the teachers called "being bold". Once we were outside we could rifle through everyone's bags and eat their lunches. We were hunter gatherers, first having to find our food. Just like dogs.

It didn't help that the teachers were as ignorant as everyone else about how to deal with us. I especially remember Mr Kearney, in his tweed coat with his stupid black hair flicked to the side, looking down on me and slapping me across the face. I also remember thinking to myself, "My father flogs we with an army belt buckle and I won't flinch for him. Do you think I'm going to flinch for you? You're fucking mad."

We bailed out the morning they put me back in baby class when I was six or seven. I'd been beaten that morning because I'd wet the bed. Then I was kicked out the door. Do you know what it's like to be kicked out the door with welts that are still burning, and it's freezing?

You're wearing some kind of baggy pants your sister wears, just cut in here and there. On your way down to school, it starts. "Hitler, Hitler. Little Hitler." We got that a lot, because my mother was German. By the time we reached school, we'd be insanely angry at everyone. Then the teacher'd start on us. All I could think was, "You expect us to learn from *you*?" They seemed pathetic.

That fateful day when I was told I was being put back a class, we reacted like the Three Musketeers. Andrew and John weren't being put back too, but we reacted as though they had. When you're triplets, it's all for one and one for all. All three of us went home.

Not long after we got there a car pulled up and dear old Mr Kearney and another teacher jumped out. They came up to the gate and started singing out, "You come back to school and we're gonna flog you."

"Fuck off. You take one step inside that gate and we'll let the dogs go."

They did. And so did we.

You should have seen the dogs go after them. One teacher headed for the hills, banging himself against one of the gate pillars. As he did, Major caught him and started pulling him down. The other teacher tried to kick Rex away. Rex got him on the leg. The teachers scrambled back to the car and I called the dogs back.

We thought it was great until a week later when they sent the van to take the dogs. Today I still feel guilty about using those dogs to get at the teachers. But they were proud soldiers, eh? When I asked them to defend me, they did exactly that. I think of them all the time … but there you go.

When Major and Rex were put down, that was the last straw. Obviously the teachers hadn't been able to get us, so they'd done the next best thing. They took the things we valued the most — our dogs.

I went back to school, but not for long. We were quietly sobbing in the corner of the classroom and Mr Kearney stood up and announced, "I think we should all have a minute's silence for the triplets' dogs." He started to laugh out loud.

I looked at the boys and said, "Not now, not now — after."

We had hurling sticks, sort of like hockey sticks only much more effective in a brawl. Andrew, John and I debated whether to just drag Kearney out of his car after school and beat him to death, but we settled on humiliating him as he'd done to us. We decided to turn his car over.

Just outside the school gates there was a kind of a cattle grid in the ground. We hid behind the pillars and as soon as he came out, we put our hurlies under his wheels and tried to use them as levers.

We were spitting at him, screaming at him. We would have killed him. Remember, we were dogs, right? He'd killed two of our pack. We had to avenge the pack right away, or more'd go down. We weren't about to let that happen for anyone.

From that day on, that man feared us. Not that that particularly concerned me. I decided I wasn't going to the school any more. I was going to hide.

I'd had it with people. Everywhere I went I heard the same thing: "He's just a bad kid." That made me even more rebellious. It also made me decide I wasn't going to have anything to do with people any more. So I went to live on the streets.

Andy and John had gone kind of straight by then. They were both starting to do pretty well at school. To be truthfully honest, when I wasn't living at home, things weren't too bad.

People were sure I'd gone insane. I lay low all day. I wouldn't come out until night-time. I wouldn't go home. Why should I? I'd only get flogged. When all the other kids had gone home, I could wander the streets. It was brilliant! You could stay up all night. You didn't have to hide from anyone

At ten I hated the world and everybody in it.

Limerick's a pretty tough old town. You have to have your wits about you and you don't have many allies. I didn't have any. I needed something that'd help me out. Because I liked dogs, I noticed this pack of stray dogs on the street. You wouldn't see them during the day, but at night they'd come out — just like I did. They'd appear at a place called the Garryowen Green.

I thought, "Gee, I'd love to be in with a group like them. I like the way they are." It was always sort of ordered in the pack. Sometimes there were a few fights and someone copped a bit of a flogging, but they weren't severe — more a know-your-place thing. Where I'd come from it was more bashing and kicking to keep you down. Those dogs had a better thing going than the humans I knew.

I knew that food was their main concern — because they were all so skinny. Up there on the hill was the slaughterhouse. It looked down over the world I'd grown to hate. But I went up there and found work. Me and a bloke called Brendan became what you might call specialists. Our specialty was to work with diseased animals. My job was to stick them in the belly. The smell was horrible. I'd open up the belly and pull the guts out. Brendan would skin them and take all the fillets and the back legs. Then I'd progress to taking the guts and the head and all that stuff, throwing them into a skip and carrying all the other meat into the back shed for salting. The meat was sold to the owners of greyhounds. The hides went for leather. The rest went for glue. That would be my gateway into the pack. I'd tee up their grub for them.

They became my pack. It's from them that I learned about the dog world — living with them, watching them, learning from them and eventually making my own contribution to the pack's wellbeing.

Humans hadn't been able to teach me anything at school, but those dogs managed to teach me about their world. I found it a lot easier to relate to their no-nonsense ways than work out the complicated world of humans. We didn't need words to communicate. They had their own way of letting everyone know the rules and I had my ADD to help me tune in to the messages they gave.

And the most important thing those dogs taught me was the one thing that I need to pass on to other people — the laws of leadership in the dog world. If you don't know what those rules are, you'll never be able to control your dog. You'll never be able to fully enjoy its company and, most important of all as far as I'm concerned, you'll never be able to do it justice.

I learned the laws of leadership from a dog called Blackie, a big Newfoundland cross thing. Jesus, he was a big dog. As far as that moth-eaten pack scrounging around the Garryowen Green was concerned, Blackie was the undisputed leader — until ten-year-old Martin McKenna, with his anger and confusion came along.

I watched Blackie and picked up on his leadership qualities, and knew I'd have to fight that black bastard. And I did. But first I drew on human resourcefulness and found a nice big stick. I suppose a lot of people will think that cruel, but look at it from *my* point of view — the point of view of a ten-year-old kid who'd abandoned all hope of ever being an acceptable human being and had sought refuge in the company of a pack of street-scavenging mongrels. You need to get down to my level, the dog level, to understand.

"You're going to mess with me, are you?" I ran after that dog and gave him the sort of hiding a real Top Dog would, so he'd never challenge my leadership again.

It worked. I won control over that pack. I became Top Dog, and, as is always the case in the dog world, I didn't just win it and maintain it by brute force. As leader it was my job to make sure the pack ate, and ate well. Working in that abattoir made me a natural for the job.

I was the only one who really knew what was going on. I knew all about the meat and I was the only one who could do anything about it. I had contacts in the trade. I even knew Max, the guard dog whose job it was to keep any intruders — human or dog — away from the meat. After all, we were workmates, eh?

I used to go back to the slaughterhouse at night and help myself to meat for my pack. The old guard dog, Max, would always be pleased to see me and sit there like he was supervising me helping myself to all that food. But I always made sure my old mate didn't get blamed for what went on. I used to snag his chain on the fence, or some other object. That way it looked as though he'd become tangled up trying to do his job.

Next morning, Brendan would turn up, find some of the meat missing and go off his brain: "You useless bastard. There's meat missing again. I'm gonna have your hide."

The old bull mastiff would sit there with a dopey look on his face, trying to work out why his boss seemed so hell bent on flogging him. I'd sing out, "Bra', for God's sake don't hit that dog. He's snagged on that piece of wire. How could he of stopped that thief?"

I could only get away with that sort of thing for so long. Eventually I decided to play smart. I became more selective in what I pinched. I took only the inside fillets and bits of each quarter of the beast, so nobody knew anything was missing. No one ever twigged. After all, I was the one who loaded it all onto the truck.

I reckon that made me the best Top Dog in the world. I was providing the food for the pack. On top of that, I'd proved I definitely wasn't scared of any big dog like Blackie. I was definitely the leader. All that territory around the abattoirs and the Garryowen Green was *mine*. People thought I was absolutely insane: "That feller's definitely lost the plot." But I hadn't.

I'd just made a conscious decision that I wasn't going to be a human. I was going to be a dog. I'd been a dog from when I was a child. I'd known it from my first. I'd always felt different. People only magnified it by their treatment of us. Andy, John and I didn't just *feel* different. We *were* different.

But that didn't worry the dog pack. They knew I was feeding them good red meat. They knew I wasn't afraid of anything. They knew I was a better leader than Blackie. Eventually even he came over. Occasionally he'd lower his head and challenge me. I'd just grab the stick and give him a whack on the head, reminding him, "I'm the leader, eh?" I always won and in the end he became a valued lieutenant.

I further cemented my position as Top Dog by protecting my fellow pack members from the powers-that-be, the council dog catchers. When we roamed around Garryowen Green at night-time, a few of the troops would start barking and people would complain to the council. If the dog catchers came around, I could provide my new pack with an area where they wouldn't get into trouble. There was a cow shed up behind the Garryowen scout hall. It wasn't used any more but it was somewhere I could throw a blanket down and that became my little house. It wasn't too bad — no one shouting and screaming, saying how stupid you were. It was all right. I wasn't afraid any more because the dogs would be there at night keeping me from trouble.

They taught me a lot. I noticed things like the fact that they weren't always sharing, and that there was always a definite line I had to keep. If I didn't, they'd all start fighting. It always started if I began to treat them as though they were humans. I only ever did that when I was missing human company, which wasn't often. But it caused total confusion. It was wrong of me. It wasn't fair to them. I was being too lax with them.

We had some great times. There were these gangs that used to come around. I was also delivering coal during the day, and the gangs would try to steal money off me. I'd have my dogs with me. I only had to threaten to sic my dogs onto them and things'd be cool.

By joining that dog pack, I'd found fellow creatures I *could* relate to, that I wasn't different from. Even today I can work out what a dog's trying to tell me. I can walk into someone's house and in less than fifteen minutes I can take their dog and it'll never worry about those people again.

I know the messages to give. They're never, "I'm unsure", or "not sure". They're always, "This is me. I'm a leader. See that chin? It's up in the air. See that chest? It's cocked out. You growl at me, I won't even look at you."

Humans always think they're better than something that's different than them because they don't understand them, and they might be better than them.

This ADD isn't an affliction. It's a different way of functioning. We can blossom into the greatest communicators in the world, so long as people are prepared to listen. Those of us with ADD who've been treated cruelly by people trying to solve or cope with it don't level any blame. But we know it doesn't work. And I know that people still make the same mistakes trying to understand and cope with their dogs.

"I'm your leader because I say so. You will obey *my* orders. You'll understand *my* ways." The poor old dog wants to say, "I don't. I *can't* understand your ways. You have to try to understand *me*. Stop beating me. Stop kicking me. Why don't you try and get down here and try to understand me?"

I remember trying to get those self-same messages across in the bad old days of my childhood. I know how it feels. But these days, I'm happy being me.

Yeah, I eventually left the abattoirs. A lot of water's gone under the bridge since I was a screwed-up ten year old. I now live an entirely different life. Who'd have thought that one day I'd be in Australia, that I'd start doing work with organisations like the Animal Welfare League in NSW, that someone from ABC Radio would hear about me, and eventually I'd be on radio actually giving people advice on how to do the right thing by their dogs?

There's been some big changes, eh? But my message is still the same, especially when it comes to dogs. They helped me find myself and I owe it to them to try and get them a better deal in this crazy old world.

When I was leaving Garryowen, I made a promise to those pack members of mine. By then I knew that I wanted more out of life than to be leader of a mob of scavengers. I took a long last look at them before I left.

"Still doing it, eh? Still scavenging out of the bins? Still skin and bones? Trust me, lads. One day I'm going to let people know what all this is really about, eh?"

So that's what I'm trying to do now. That's what being the Dogman is all about. One day I want to go back to Garryowen and show them all, people *and* dogs, that I've found a better way of existing together. And that other people are finally starting to sit up and take notice.

chapter 2

become a real leader

Give your dog dog-ocracy, not democracy

Thinking and acting like a dog is wonderful — it's simple. Human beings like to complicate things a lot. We can't expect a dog to understand our complicated ways. Now, I'm not anything special, right? All I am is a kind of a translator, from the dog to the human.

Well, at the moment I see us humans as having our lines crossed a bit when it comes to understanding and communicating with dogs. And when we humans can't understand something we get frustrated and angry — and that's not the way to go because one of us will end up in the pound. And it's never the human, it's always the dog, you know?

What's going wrong between humans and dogs?

We give our dogs democracy when DOG-OCRACY is what they really want. This is the only system they understand. They don't understand fairness and sharing and doing everything for their buddies. That's not how they work. That's not how Mother Nature designed them.

They have a different way. In the Dog World they have a system where at the very top of their Ladder is the Leader and his rule reaches right down through everyone in the pack. Everyone in the pack has their own position, and nobody ever shares their rung of the ladder with anybody else. Everybody defends their position, and if anything, tries to get up a little higher. Some dogs are born to try and climb a little harder than others. They're more ambitious, hey? So there is very little sharing or fairness in their world. What the Leader says the pack does. The pack just does it. There's no shared decision making or courts of justice where one dog can say, "Hey! That's not fair! That's not fair!"

Life in a dog pack *isn't* fair by our standards but they don't care about that — they care about survival.

Imagine if there *was* democracy in the dog world? It'd be a right bloody shambles. Could you imagine a pack of dogs sitting down, looking around at each other and having a committee meeting about where they were going to go hunting that night?

Can you imagine it? The pack would all starve and the prey would have all died of old age or moved on by the time these dogs got it together enough to go out hunting. Even worse, what if the committee meeting exploded into an argument? Dogs have got big teeth and some committee members would end up getting attacked and the pack wouldn't be able to hunt successfully — there would be key members missing. Again the pack would starve. So that's why dogs don't have democracy. Mother Nature was concerned more with dogs surviving as a species than their individual feelings getting hurt. But dogs don't care because their own system, dog-ocracy, works wonderfullly for them.

The Leader makes a decision — the pack does it. That's it. That's how simple the Dog World really is.

How are leaders made?

If you want to be Leader of your pack and always have your dog obey you, then you've got to make sure you're right at the TOP of the Ladder. But how do you climb up there? Well, just like all good dog leaders — including Black Dog, King of the Garryowen Strays — we humans are going to have to win all the Leadership Rules of the Dog World every day.

Luckily, these are really simple rules. By constantly winning each one of them every day, we earn the right to be Leader of the pack. As soon as we stop bothering to win them — and go, "Bugger this! I'm gonna let my bloody dog do whatever it wants!", our dog will see us as an incompetent Leader and so will start challenging our position at the top of the Ladder.

If he wins enough of the Leadership Rules on a regular basis, then he thinks, "Right! I'm the best Leader around here — I'm at the top. Great! I love it up here. *Once I get up here I don't have to do anything unless I want to.*"

Aha! Sound familiar?

Yep! Most dogs out there believe they're the Leader of their human pack. That is the main reason why dogs won't behave for us — not because they're being bold or mean or selfish or ungrateful or stupid — but because in their eyes we haven't yet earned the right to tell them what to do.

And how do we earn that right? We use the Leadership Rules every day. We choose consistency over chaos.

Now I know that all ye out there reading this book can do the same as me when I was just a wild, street kid. You too can make yourself a good Leader of your own pack, just as I did back in Garryowen with those stray dogs, and just as I do now with my own two dogs, Jack and Fianna.

So here, in the following pages, are the Leadership Rules and they're simple. Relax! Everything about the Dog World is nice and simple, that's why I love dealing with 'em so much.

the leadership rules

Rule 1

The Leader always eats first. Why? Because the Leader went out and got the food. So when do we feed our dog? LAST. Tie him up outside, make him sit. If he won't sit, keep turning away until he will. Once he's sitting, pretend to eat his food, drop it down as though you've had enough of it and walk away. Your job is done. You've just fulfilled the most important Leadership Rule of the day.

Give your dog about fifteen minutes to eat the food. If he hasn't eaten it, have a string tied to the bowl and pull it away. Remember, he's still tied by his leash. Why pull the food away? Because the Leader would always come back and eat it himself.

Rule 2

The Leader tells everyone what to do because he understands the rules best and provides the food regularly. That's a good enough reason, isn't it? Well, in the dog world it is. Don't allow your dog to rule the household. The problem section is full of ways you can stop him doing this.

Rule 3

The Leader always makes sure he is the centre of attention. No sharing the limelight here — this is a solo act. So don't be paying attention to the dog all the time. It's only confusing him into believing that he is the Leader and that can get him into big trouble.

Rule 4

The Leader always takes control when something unusual happens. This might be a stranger arriving at your house, a strange dog walking past, a sudden noise outside. Once your dog has alerted you that something unusual is happening, call him to you with a tidbit, clip him on the leash next to his Magic Rug, a rug that you have ready next to a leash. So once clipped on, he can't get off the rug. If your dog refuses to come, get the leash and go and clip it on him and then drag him back to his Magic Rug — we mean what we say as the Leader. "It is our right to investigate, Dog, not yours."

Rule 5

The Leader always has to win any games being played, so only play the games you can win. These could be tricks. "You do a trick for me and I'll give you a tidbit and praise. I got you to do something for me so I won that game." Another game is Fetch the Ball. Always make sure we win the ball again by using a tidbit — "You give me the ball, I give you the tidbit. I win again. See how easy I can beat you?" Now take your trophy and put it in a drawer until the next game.

Dangerous games we don't play: Tug-of-war, wrestling, play-biting, chase and jump up. These are all things dogs would do if they were killing food or fighting an opponent. We're not food and we definitely don't want to be an opponent, especially our children.

So no compromise here, they just can't play them. The law won't compromise when it comes to putting your dog down for biting. We know all too well what dogs can do with their teeth if they really want to win one day. Remember, your dog can play these dangerous games with another dog which is a good reason to get a second dog of the opposite sex.

Rule 6

A Leader can take food off weaker pack members. How? He stares at them until they drop it. So never let your dog take any food off a child unsupervised. Otherwsie we're setting our child up for a potential bite. Remember there will come a day when your kid will not want to give up what it wants to the dog and then your dog may believe it has the right to bite the child to give up the food.

Under adult supervision your child may give your dog a tidbit by getting the dog to sit, pretending to eat the food, letting it slip through their fingers at the dog's feet and walking away.

Rule 7

A Leader uses body postures to prove he is dominant over you. Some popular ones are: leaning against you, standing on your feet, lifting his chin really high while he sits up tall, standing frozen over you while you're sitting or lying down, jumping up so his paws go on your chest. This also includes lying on your lap.

Start recognising dominant postures and don't allow your dog to do them to anyone, especially children.

Rule 8

Lead dogs have right of way through any entrances and exits. How can we stop our dog doing this? Clip him on his leash and if he goes to push past you through the door, close the door firmly, making sure not to hurt your dog in the process. We only want the shock value — not pain. So always make sure everyone goes through the door before your dog.

Rule 9

The Leader always has the most comfortable and important resting and sleeping spots. So don't let your dog on any couch, chair or bed. Remember, if you try to share these with your dog, he'll quickly give you his version of sharing and take over. If you want your dog to have a bed or couch, give him a doggy basket of his own and put it on the floor. If you can't keep him off these things, clip him next to a Magic Rug.

Rule 10

The Leader never gets out of the way for anyone. So no more tippy-toeing around your dog. We're not asking for right of way, we're taking it. In future, if your dog won't get out of your way, barge through him as though you didn't see him. Say nothing. If he's lying down, do the Harlem Shuffle. Shuffle your feet noisily towards the dog, without looking down at him as that will only give the game away. Shuffle into the coat of his hair and he'll quickly get up out of the way. Again say nothing, acting as if we knew he was going to get out of our way anyway.

The leadership rules — a summary

1 **Make sure your dog always eats LAST.**
2 **Don't allow your dog to rule the household. He makes no more demands. He does everything you say without exception.**
3 **Don't make your dog the centre of attention.**
4 **Don't let your dog take control whenever anything unusual happens, like when strangers come to the house, a dog walks past or there's a strange noise outside.**
5 **Don't let your dog win any games. If you play fetch the ball, always keep final possession of the ball. Don't play dangerous games like wrestling, tug-of-war, chase and jump up and play-biting as these all teach your dog to bite.**
6 **Don't let your dog take food off children. Learn the safe way to supervise your child giving your dog a tidbit.**
7 **Don't allow your dog to use dominant postures over any human, especially children.**
8 **Don't let your dog control entrances and exits.**
9 **Don't let your dog rest or sleep on the couch, chair or bed.**
10 **Don't let dogs block your way. Learn how to move them out of your way without using any aggression.**

The main thing you have to remember with the Leadership Rules is that *every* human in the household — no matter what size or age — is more important than the dog. Give him everything *last*. Out of everybody, always give him the *least desirable thing*. Notice him the least. If everyone in the household follows these rules consistently, your dog will live a long, stress-free life with you.

This is not cruel to your dog. It simply means that Dog, you put in the least amount to this pack. You don't successfully hunt and provide for us. You didn't provide this comfortable den. Therefore, Dog, you don't mind being at the bottom of our pack. That's the way it is in the Dog's World — whoever does the least is at the bottom. They are certainly never the Leader.

Using the Dog Leadership Rules

Become more observant. Start watching your dog discreetly and start recognizing when he's challenging anyone in your pack for the leadership. Stop all challengers calmly, confidently and immediately.

Make sure your dog is right at the bottom of the pack. Don't allow your dog to think he's dominant over the children or the baby or even the visitors. Because they might have a bit of trouble winning the challenges, it's up to you, the owner and good Pack Leader, to ensure that the dog clearly understands no human is lower ranking than himself, no matter how small and helpless. I go into more detail about kids and dogs in the problem solving section of this book.

Be a consistent leader. For years I've seen people train their dogs down at the Saturday morning dog training classes. For an hour or so each week they get their dog to sit, heel, stay and what have you in a place far from the den. Whenever I see this, I can't help picturing an imaginary Lead Dog taking his pack down to the local park to put them through their paces.

The idea sounds a little silly, doesn't it? The lead dog doesn't need to train his pack for an hour or so each week — he simply *is* the Leader at all times. He is Leader inside the den. He is Leader around the pack territory. He is Leader out on the hunt. If at any time he does not act like a Leader, then any ambitious members of his pack will quickly grab the opportunity to start challenging him.

So if you really want to have an obedient dog, make sure you are the Leader *at all times*. In the house. In the garden. Down at the park. Out on the walk. Down at the beach. In the car. When visitors come over. When people walk past your house. When you're talking to your neighbours over the fence. *Everywhere — but most especially in the den*. In the Dog World the den is a very powerful place to win challenges. Win them here and you'll be a very strong Leader.

How long will all this take? This will depend on a few things. Are you really being as consistent as possible applying *all* the Dog Leadership Rules? Or are you insisting your dog respects you as Leader sometimes but not bothering at other times? If so, your dog believes he has every right to challenge you for the leadership. He obviously has more perseverance then you.

Are *all* the members of your family following the Leadership Rules? If everyone isn't consistently keeping the dog at the bottom of the pack, he'll find it's well worth challenging for the leadership constantly. After all, if he's winning against two or three pack members then he's probably half way to the Leadership already.

Are you giving your dog enough exercise? Especially if you own an energetic breed. A bored dog bursting with energy has vast amounts of time to devote to challenging everyone for the leadership. I've never heard a truer saying than, "A tired dog is a well behaved dog."

Are you being a good Leader? Is it nice for your dog being at the bottom of the pack? If your dog can't depend on you for a calm, enjoyable routine each day he might start challenging you. Maybe he can do a better job as Leader, or so he thinks.

Don't use violence to win challenges. Otherwise your dog will start thinking, "Hey! In this pack we use violence to prove our dominance over other members." Once we start heading down this road, it's hard to turn back. Who's to say your dog won't follow your example of using physical punishment and nip your child or grandkid one day when they accidentally let him win a few challenges? Unlike dogs we have human brain power to help us always win any challenge our dog throws our way.

Remember, success lies in your attitude. You really have to believe you're the leader. You could follow my ideas after reading this book but if you don't really believe you're acting like a Leader, then you're not going to enjoy much success.

Your dog will be watching this new you very carefully. As soon as he senses you have any doubts about what you're doing he'll think, "Ah, you've finally worked out how to become Leader — but I'm gonna keep testing you and testing you and testing you some more until I find out exactly how confident a Lead Dog you are. Maybe you'll give it up after a few weeks if I keep on challenging you. It's certainly worth a try, isn't it?"

dogs for all seasons

If you're serious about trying your hand at being a Top Dog, you better start paying closer attention to the four-legged members of your pack. Even after you accept that they're not people, dogs aren't just dogs. I mean, hey, you don't have to be a genius to work out that they're all shapes, sizes, temperaments and character. To really be a Top Dog, you'll have to adapt your approach to every type.

Small dogs

Let's start with little dogs. They're all very active and the one thing you should avoid is over-stimulating them. If you do, you're falling into the trap of giving them exactly what they want. Being very active is a great way of getting their own way. They get worked up into such a state that you haven't a hope in hell of keeping up with them. In the end, you give up and leave them to their own devices — like I said, exactly what they want you to do. They know they're free to do whatever they want.

So don't excite little dogs. They specialise in getting their own way by creating havoc. That's why they keep running round from person to person. When everyone's totally confused, the dog feels it's won. It thinks it's in control. It *knows* it's in control.

Picking them up

Don't ever pick up little dogs. Being picked up gives them a sense of being who they are absolutely *not* — and that is a leader. They just see you as a slave. If you're willing to pick up your puppy or dog, and walk around with them, all they see is that you're there to do exactly what they want.

Look at it from the way the dog sees you treating your kids. They're seven or eight years old. They're pretty heavy, and they don't want to be carried around anyway. But you're picking up your pup or your small dog. You can't blame the little dog for thinking that you regard him as more important than your kids.

The dog already knows that you're prepared to pay more attention to it than you do to your kids. If a child nags you, you can always say, "Go away and do something else." But invariably when a little dog wants attention, you'll drop what you're doing and give it. They're more active and more persistent than your kids in seeking your attention, anyway.

It is pretty hard to ignore a cute little dog going through its attention-grabbing paces. The minute you bend down and tell it to calm down, you've blundered into its net. You're doing exactly what it wants. And when it jumps into your arms you think, "Oh, it's so cute. I'll just walk around with it."

The sad fact is that once you pick that dog up or sit it on your lap, you're telling it to dominate you. Little dogs don't need much to tell them to dominate. They'll do it much quicker than a big dog.

I know grannies especially love little dogs. They're victims of a great con act. Little dogs have grannies nailed to the floor. I've been to houses where the grannies have had little dogs that constantly bailed them up, consistently wrecking their lives and running the place.

The solution's clear. Don't pick them up. Don't pay so much

attention to them. Don't sook them. Remember, they're not a pet. They're a little pack member.

Pick me! Pick me!

Little dogs are great ones for using their paws a lot and scraping you. Of course it's an attempt at grabbing attention. What you don't do is look down. That's exactly what the little dog wants. If you fold your arms and hold them up high, the little dog can't see your face. When a dog can't see you it can't interact and it'll quickly learn to stop scraping.

Bedroom secrets

Don't let little dogs in your bedroom. That's lethal. Little dogs seem to love the bedroom more than anything.

I don't know why, but that's when I'm called in. It's never when the dog's just messing around in the kitchen.

From the dog's point of view, the bedroom's a great place to hang out. It's warm and comfortable and safe. People tend to let them jump up on the bed and sleep with them simply by virtue of them being small. "It's okay. He doesn't take up much space." But you watch out how much space that little dog *really* takes.

Then it starts thinking, "Okay I'll divide up the humans in their bed." When that happens you're really in trouble, eh? Little dogs are great at dividing and ruling. I deal with this later in the book where we discuss problem solving, but basically, don't let them up on the bed.

They might act all cutey cutey: "Oh, look at me. Couldn't you just let me up?" But their innocence is just a cover for terrorising you for the rest of your life. Remember, as cute as they might seem, little dogs are often more of a dog than a big dog. They *have* to be because they have to learn to bluff more just to survive. They have to exaggerate everything. A big dog doesn't worry as much. It doesn't feel as stressed. It does less thinking because it's got different functions.

Gotcha!

Little dogs snap a lot. The main reason is that a lot of them were ratters, back when they were functional dogs. A chow in China, a Jack Russell in England, or an Irish terrier in Ireland, they were all snappers to kill rats and other small prey. Again, I'll deal with it in detail later, but snapping can be a problem, especially if you have children.

Often, when you put your hand over a little dog to pat it, it goes to snap at you.

"Jesus! Snappy little bugger, aren't you?"

He's not. It's just that he's so small and you're so big and you're in such a major dominant position he thinks, "All I can do now is defend myself and snap." Big dogs, when that hand goes over, don't find it so, so it's not much of a problem.

Meet the kids

A big dog will usually take a bit more punishment from children than will a little dog. Being smaller, the little dog might be pushier, but deep down, it knows it hasn't got the guns to back it up. In that case, the little dog will resort to violence. Sure, there's no logic to it, but like I said earlier, dogs don't know logic.

Never leave *any* dog alone with children, but especially don't leave little dogs alone with them — because they're snappier. They're likely to attack anything that moves on instinct, whereas a larger dog doesn't have that instinct.

G'day Digger

Little dogs dig a lot. They're not terriers for nothing — *terra* being the Latin word for the earth. It means they're digging dogs. Big dogs aren't. Little dogs are used to going into holes to catch things. A big dog won't. Back in time, a big dog'd be out on the plain catching something. A little dog would get a mole, mouse or a rat.

It's unfortunate, really, because people who buy small dogs often do it because they have a good garden and don't want it destroyed. "If I get a big dog, he'll wreck the place. A little dog never would. I'll take my little dog out gardening with me, digging up weeds and planting pots and all that."

The little dog's looking at you. When you go inside, he thinks, "Jesus. He never found the bones. I'll go and find them for him." Next thing, the dog's digging up all over your rose garden and you're screaming, "Jesus Christ! What are you doing?"

The dog looks up at you and goes, "Nup, I couldn't find the bones either."

What else do you expect him to think? You'd been out there hunting for bones that you buried before and now you can't find them. He's a specialised little digger and is quite prepared to dig to China to find those bones, eh? The dog has no idea or concept about your beautiful rose garden.

You can understand the owner wanting to kill that dog — metaphorically speaking, of course. He just didn't understand what was going on. The trouble is, you can bet your life there *are* people who like their garden more than they like their dog. Their little dog does something that they don't understand and that little dog will quickly be in the pound.

All dogs need to be dogs. The problem is, people don't allow them to be dogs. Of course dogs dig. They dig for bones. They dig if it's hot, to get down in the cool earth. They dig to eat some roots. They dig because they're bored. They dig because there's a smell under there. Or they dig because they dig.

But what does it matter *why* they dig? Deal with your problem by giving them their own little digging area. What you're saying then, is, "Keep digging. I'll send down a rope to pull you up after. No worries, eh?"

It makes sense to provide your dog with an area of its own where it can do all that stuff. You can bury some bones in it, put some nice smells there and fence it off. That way, whenever you want to do some gardening, you can put your little digger in there. The dog will sniff and think, "There's something buried here." It can dig and chew to its heart's content and keep whatever it gets out of the ground. It's gardening.

Energetic dogs

These blokes get their way by simply wearing you down. Please, please, *please* remember a cattle dog does *not* belong in a suburban back yard. A collie does not belong in a suburban back yard. A kelpie doesn't belong in a suburban back yard.

They're different kinds of dogs again. They're used to running sixty, eighty, one hundred kilometres a day, then being chained back at their 44 gallon drum and left there until the next morning.

So if you want an energetic dog, be an energetic person yourself. That's one of the major things to look out for. They can destroy your life for want of exercise.

Invariably I find people only bought a working dog because they liked the colour of its coat. They didn't bother to find out anything about it — what sort of exercise it would need, what it would do, what stimulation it needed, or whatever. That's why you have cattle dogs and other energetic breeds living in back yards in total misery.

You might think, "Oh, he runs around the back yard." A back yard isn't a big enough exercise area. In the wild, a back yard's like the place where everyone lies down. It's the den. Nobody gets excited around there.

That's why the owner of an energetic dog needs to be energetic themselves. And you have to have the time to spend with that sort of dog. If you don't, if you only bought the dog because of the way it looked and the happy smile on its face, the smile on *your* face will quickly become a scowl when that dog totally badgers you and uses its energy level against you.

Big dogs

People, being what they are, are just as likely to get things arse-about with big dogs too. A lot of people say, "My big dog is pretty clumsy. He's always leaning on me. He's always stepping on my toes. He never gets out of the way." They think of their big dog as clumsy and stupid. But it's not.

A big dog is not clumsy. A big dog is not stupid. A big dog is not short-sighted. It knows exactly what it's doing. It's using its weight to gently push you out of the way. "I'm testing you."

If my dog leans on me I get something sharp and just pinch him. Nothing nasty. I just pinch his skin. He yowls and runs away. "Well Jack, that's what happens when you lean on me, matey. Don't try that one on me, I know what you're trying to do. You're trying to dominate me in using what you have — just like the little dog did with the paws and all the yapping and that."

The big dog uses something different. It's always bumping us. It's constantly bumping over the children.

Say, for example, you come home. The first thing you see is the dog as he comes barging through the kitchen. You say, "Jesus, you're a clumsy bloody dog." But you still pat him. That's exactly why the dog did it. He barged through the children first to say, "This is my way of showing I'm better and higher ranking than them and I deserve to be patted first."

Ouch!

Big dogs step on your toes a lot. They lie around a lot. They lie across doorways and they're constantly blocking your way. You think, "You bludging lazy dog. You never get out of my way."

It won't because it thinks it has the right to. It's a big dog. "It takes me too long to get up and, anyway, seeing I'm the leader, why should I?"

Dealing with it is pretty simple. You just pay back in kind. If your big dog steps on your toes, you step on his. It's not going to hurt you as much as it hurts him. And when you're around the dog, stamp your feet. Whenever I get close to my dogs I do a bit of stamping. The dogs know what it means. "Stay the hell out of my way. Don't bump into me, don't come too close unless you want your toes stepped on."

No detour

Similarly, if they keep lying down around you and not getting out of your way, do the Harlem shuffle. Just shuffle straight into them.

If my dog's lying down and I'm carrying something, I know he has no intention of getting up. I keep shuffling into him, pinching his hair and his skin. I won't look down at him. What I'm saying is, "I'm the leader here and I have the right of passage wherever I go." Only the leader can stop anyone and only the leader doesn't get out of the way — not for anything or anyone.

If I say, "Hang on, Rover. I'll get around you," he's thinking, "Yes, I'm the leader, so you better do that, eh?"

No way, buddy.

Paying the toll

Big dogs especially like to lie across big doorways because it's like a toll bridge. Anyone who passes has to pay a sort of tribute — recognising the dog's dominance by letting it get away with what it's doing. After all, the dog's giving out pretty strong signals which other dogs have no trouble understanding: "You have to either step over me or go around me. Oh, you stopped to pat me, eh? That's the fee you have to pay for the right to pass by."

The doorway's like the entrance to the den and the true leader has the right to decide who goes in and out, who moves out of the way for whom. By doing those sorts of things, big dogs are cleverly using what they've got in the same way that little dogs and excited dogs do. No dog abstracts things like people do. They don't dream and fantasise about how they'd like things to be. They just use whatever they have to get their own way.

Whoops!

Ever noticed how big dogs like to barge into you when running up to you? Here's a trick. What I do when that happens is lift my knees up high and raise my hands. You watch my big dog veer away. It knows for a fact that it's getting more than it's giving and it's confused.

Running into and barging into things is what a large dog always did to knock its prey over before killing it, or unbalancing a foe in a fight. That's fairly savage stuff he adapted to bully you into submission. But when you raise your arms with your knees up high, you look like a tank to him.

It also reduces his ability to bluff you. He can't see your eyes and when he can't do that, he can't pull the wool over them. He's confused. "Christ, I can't see his eyes. What the hell's going on?" It's usually confusing enough for him to give up, lie down or go away.

And when I do that I haven't resorted to violence, eh? I've just messed with that dog's head.

Slow motion

Barging, leaning, stepping on you or lazing around are tricks big dogs use to get their own way. But something they're often unfairly accused of doing is feigning slowness. Big dogs aren't always the nippiest things on four legs. I've often heard people say, "He's trying to put it over me, I know he is."

No he's not. He's a big dog. He's got big bones. He can't just spring up like a little dog. He's got to take his time getting up. He's got to make sure that he doesn't pull a tendon, trap a nerve or something. If he does, he can't go to the physio. He's dead. He can't hunt, he can't walk. He's weak. Nobody wants weakness in the pack, so they flick him off. What's love got to do with it?

Not so much of the woof!

Big dogs rarely bark. Little dogs are more demanding in their barking than big dogs. A little dog thinks he needs more backup in a confrontation — real or imagined. A big dog rarely needs backup.

While we're on barking … people are always saying their dog barks at night.

"Where do you put him at night?"

"Out the front."

Jesus, no wonder he barks. When you do that, you're putting him on sentry duty. And when he's left way out front on his own, in the dark, he thinks you're saying, "There's no backup for you, dog." And being on sentry duty, he feels you've already given him his orders. You've told him, "If anything comes down that street, bark and let me know."

When he does, he's likely to get a flogging. The dog thinks, "Get it right, man. If you want me off duty put me out the back."

The dog is always less likely to bark out the back than he is out front. Why? There's no road out the back. There's no people walking out the back. They're all walking out the front.

I've seen and heard some stupidity lately from so-called experts claiming a dog needs a view — it must be able to see the road and all that sort of stuff. What a joke. If the dog can see the street and all its activity, of course it's going to get stirred up and of course it's going to bark. It may even go that little bit further, and leap the fence and take things into its own hands, or should I say, "Own jaws".

Guard dog garbage

There seems to be this widespread belief that big dogs are guard dogs. They're not — not all of them, any way. Labradors are pretty big. Golden retrievers are big. But they're pretty docile.

Make no mistake about it. All dogs will attack you. Any dog, from a fearful dog to an excited dog, to a happy dog. So let's be quite clear about that first, because people tend to think that only big dogs and guard dogs bite.

The truth is that size does matter, but not in the way people think. A medium-sized dog like a collie is more likely to bite you than a big German shepherd. A German shepherd is more confident.

And yes, the danger increases as size decreases. A little dog is even more likely to take a chunk out of you. The only difference is a big dog will do more damage when it bites. So when you hear about a big dog that bites, he's invariably called a guard dog.

Bred to bite

The crazy thing is that when a so-called guard dog bites someone and everyone gets scandalised, the poor old dog is only doing the very thing it has been trained to do. Yet the guard dog wears all the blame.

If you train a dog to bite someone, never mind if you think that person's a villain or not, that dog is just as likely to turn around and bite you. If you psyche it up to do all the defending, fronting up and attacking for you, isn't it only right that the dog thinks it's the leader instead of you? "Hey man, I'm out here doing the fighting. I must be doing the loving too, eh? I'll take your bitch off you and you can go back up the line." Crude and nasty? Well *that's* the way dogs think.

The majority of people who buy guard dogs *have* to be afraid of something, no matter how tough or macho many of them try to look and act. No confident person buys a guard dog. They put on their camouflage trousers and combat boots and train those dogs up to attack and bite and call them great dogs.

The trouble is, that dog *is* great and knows that its owner is weak, because it can *sense* the lack of confidence. That dog will now put it over that owner as much as it would any stranger. So the very dog that owner bought to protect him is now a danger to him. A dog like that will stand up to strangers at first, then it'll take on its owner. I've seen it time and time again.

Dogs don't need much encouragement to attack, especially when attacking is seen as a rewarding thing. People who train guard and attack dogs usually give them food for doing that type of stuff.

Then there's the kids ...

Of course, worse than your dog turning on you is when they attack your children. The combination of an attack dog and kids is an absolute recipe for disaster. Any dog that's been taught that it's rewarding to bite will probably go and bite your child, and come back looking for a tidbit.

Children are always getting bitten by dogs. Often it dates back to the dog's puppy days, when everyone thought how cute and how much fun it was to play-fight with the pup. Play-fighting is the same as attack training. A funny, cute way of attacking or a serious way — it's all the same. A funny way is only an excited start to a really aggressive attack.

When the kid acts rough, the puppy thinks, "Hey, you act rougher than me. I'll remember that." Later when the dog is *much* bigger, it recalls, "How did I get what I wanted as a puppy? I bit you." It becomes a life skill. The dog learns to communicate by biting and bullying, rather than the time-honoured system of body signals.

Macho men

Rotties and Dobermans love to jump up on people's backs. Men who own big dogs are constantly going, "Come on up here, Rover. Put your paws up here on my chest," and all that kind of stuff.

Why the hell do they do it? The dog already knows it's dominating them and yet they've got the dog up there, wrestling with it. The dog thinks it's all a game. In the very near future it's going to start biting anyone it wants to, because it's been taught that it's *fun*.

And in the wild dog world it probably is. Dogs do play-fight in their world and it is fun to them. But don't forget they've got a greater pain tolerance than people — a lot greater. They bite too hard for humans. It might be a game for the dog, but it's still hurting you, or your child, or your unsuspecting member of the general public.

Rottweilers are especially formidable dogs. They get that giddy excitedness about them. Then their eyes suddenly change and they're up on your back trying to bite your neck. Those dogs really mean business when they're given the opportunity.

See you in court

On top of all that, if you have a guard dog and you've taken the trouble to have it trained, you stand a good chance of losing everything if it bites someone — even an intruder. That's what the law says. The police are there to protect society from villains — not you and your dog.

It's highly likely that if a criminal can prove that the dog that attacked him had been trained, it's proof that you gave that dog intent. When your dog attacked, you were breaking the law. At best, if the dog *hasn't* been trained and someone invades your home and gets bitten they can't sue you. That dog was just protecting the den, protecting the pack.

"Beware — guard dog" signs tell the world you've trained that dog to attack and if he jumps the fence and bites someone, you're in strife. So what have you got now? A dangerous dog that'll bite anything and anyone; who'll dominate everyone, who'll terrorise everyone in the family. Even when you're playing it will suddenly become aggressive. All you can ever do is back down.

Why anyone would consider risking playing a game with a dog like that is beyond me, but they do. The dog knows the owner's basically weak. Rough games give it the go-ahead to play just as rough, and even rougher with all and sundry.

It's like a gun primed to go off at any time. Even the poor old dog itself doesn't know when that's likely to occur. It might be better if it could, but any reaction could trigger its dark side.

Let me get back to that point again. When you've bought the guard dog because you're afraid, you now have something to *really* be afraid of — the dog. And with good reason. It's stronger and more aggressive than you. It ignores you. It's worked out just where it stands in the pack — at the top. Remember, this isn't an intelligent democracy. It's the dog world.

So what do I say to people who want a guard dog? Don't!

Better a barker

If someone's going to rob your house and they hear a dog barking, they'll go down the road and rob another house — it's as simple as that. It mightn't lower the crime rate, but it lets you off the hook.

When you attack-train a dog, it's less likely to bark. I know. I've trained attack dogs when I was younger. Why does it need to bluff now? It's been given the go-ahead to do the real thing.

Attack dogs can just lie in wait to kill the next piece of prey that comes along. And they like it. It gives them a sense of power — of being Top Dog. "If I want something, I bite. If I'm unsure, I'll bite."

The dog has always been taught to bite. It knows that biting you will get you to do what it wants. You are now under siege in your own home. In the generally illogical world of dogs there's logic in biting. Biting gets control and order. I don't think one child or one human is worth a hundred dogs. We made the mistake, we have to rectify it.

It's probably too late to train it out of them. Violence is a very, very powerful thing. It proves that you're a leader. The only way out for people who have dogs like that is to have them put down. Ninety per cent of the time, guard dogs bite innocent people ... and die for their trouble. The majority of dogs that are attack trained will never get the opportunity to bite a real intruder. The same percentage are put down for biting family members or innocent bystanders.

Remember, if you've taught the dog to attack strangers, you've made everyone else out there a potential target. How do you think your dog feels when you take it out amongst other people? "I'm afraid of that person. I'll bite them."

Pit bulls, German shepherds, dobermans, mastiffs — they're

all good dogs. I have nothing against them. But they only stay good dogs if you know what their capability is — and you stay the leader. Those types of dogs need to be trained *not* to bite. They're predisposed to biting. They know they're big. They know they're strong. They know they've got big teeth. They know they can bluff you and scare you.

All the biting and attacks come from the misconception that a guard dog will make you safe. You're not safe. You're in more danger now than you've ever been before.

Are you serious? You've gone and trained an attack dog and you don't know his rules? What's to stop him biting you every time he thinks you're doing something wrong?

My dog would never do that stuff!

Maybe not, but the potential is always there and that's why you must be aware of it. When it's too late, it's no good apologising to the world and telling people that your rampaging Rottweiler was only playing. Shame on you! You should never put a dog in that position.

Most people just look at big dogs and immediately they're afraid. The dog thinks, "Why am I smelling fear off you? If you're afraid then you're going to try to do something bad to me first. I'm going to get aggressive with you *now*." If you were more confident around big dogs, they would be more confident about you.

You really don't need to train large dogs. The sheer size of them is enough to deter anybody. And if you were being attacked, your dog would defend you naturally. It was attacking long before humans came along.

Mixed breeds

Cross a golden retriever with a terrier and you'll get a dog that wants to go into the water, drop to the bottom and dig holes. I know that's extreme, but it illustrates the point I want to make about mixed messages in the dog world.

I can't prove it, but nor can all those professors with their new technology disprove it, but I believe such dogs have competing drives within them that are constantly telling them to do different things. It's okay, as long as you understand it.

It probably doesn't become a problem unless you've got something like a pit bull mixed with a labrador. A labrador's a placid type of dog and that's probably what you first see when he's playing with you. Then the dog reaches a certain level of excitement and the pit bull kicks in. Suddenly he's not acting like a labrador. "Now I'm *really* ready for battle."

The outcasts

Although most dogs kept as pets might be of mixed breeding, people seem to rarely prefer them. They'd much rather have pedigreed dogs. Mixed bred dogs are the last to be picked. I've heard one theory that people who don't fit in themselves go for mixed breeds.

Whatever the real situation, it's all okay, providing you realise what you have to deal with. You must realise you have to deal with at least two dogs and know what they're bred from. You could have a cattle dog crossed with a German shepherd. The cattle dog will go rounding up, but the German shepherd will eventually take over and attack to kill. "Oh, I'm having so much fun running around." Then, "Bugger off, I'm in my German shepherd stage now and I'm going to pull my prey down and kill it!"

There are a lot of good dogs out there, but there's also bad situations ready to happen. People don't seem to want to know about them. They know more about the wildlife in Africa than they do about their dog in the back yard. Although it's the dog in the back yard that bites more people than the lion out there in the wild, people fear the lion more.

They wouldn't go near that lion but they mess about with dogs with big sharp teeth and think they're pets.

chapter 4

the cute years

It might make sense to you to recognise that the best way to establish your credentials as Top Dog is to get in early and strike when your dog seems most vulnerable — when it's a puppy. Like all human logic, it's not necessarily that simple. Sure, you stand a better chance of imprinting your authority on a pup, but those tens of thousands of years of dog evolution got in well before your ancestors were walking upright. Dogs' rules predate humans' by several millennia.

Just because a puppy's smaller, cuddlier and cuter doesn't mean you can take things for granted. There are things you can do to make it realise you're the leader. But it's not as easy as it may sound. You've got to do them properly.

Do what Mammy says

Basically, when a puppy's born, it has to do what Mammy says. If it doesn't, it doesn't get fed. And if it disobeys again, it gets eaten. It becomes food.

There are very clear laws in the dog world that say, "You can't make any independent decisions on our own."

"I'll feed you when I'm ready."

"Don't go round and hassle the hell out of me."

Those rules are so definite and so strongly and effectively enforced that by the time the puppy's about six weeks old, it's completely learned everything it will ever need to know about being a puppy and a dog. It's been around other pups in its litter. So the idea that dogs don't get to socialise with other dogs early on isn't right. From the very first moment, they're learning about who's higher ranking and who's where in the pack. They already have their own little pack structure and in it, everyone knows their position.

Then you, the well-meaning owner stumble in and stuff it all up.

The big change

First of all, you take that puppy away from the Mammy and cart it home. At only six weeks of age, the usual minimum age people tend to get pups, a big change has suddenly come into its previously strict but well-ordered existence. Before then, the puppy would never have had so much importance forced on it. Man, it's different from now on.

The first thing you do to it is pick it up and carry it home. You cuddle it in the car. You pay it all the attention in the world and everyone comes running around it, right? They're all looking at it, wanting it and touching it. That's fine but only if it's very brief.

But most people don't know that. The puppy becomes the centre of everyone's attention for too long. Everyone keeps doing it. "It's my turn to play with the puppy!"

"No, I want to hold it."

"He can sit on my lap."

You can't blame the puppy for immediately accepting that it is the centre of attention. It must be more important than anyone else. People are feeding it and always going to it. Others are always trying to take it from whoever's currently playing with it.

If it has a free moment, someone in the family decides they can't afford to wait for the puppy to go to them. They want it and they want it *now*! So they run to it and pick it up.

If a person walks into the room and sees the pup lying there and there's other people there (members of the pack), that person goes straight to the puppy. "Hello, puppy. How's it going?" They probably don't even acknowledge anybody else in the room.

So people are constantly giving this message to the puppy: "You are very important. Everybody in this pack pays attention to you. Everybody in this pack comes to you. Everybody in this pack lifts you up all the time."

No wonder it gets ideas above its station.

Deadly playtime

The next ill-advised step in this whole procedure involves playtime. "Come on, puppy. Let's have a game!"

And what games do people pick? They play little wrestle games with it. "Ahh, watch him do this." They get the puppy down. It's growling and play-fighting. Everybody's laughing and giggling. The pup's leg's grabbed.

"Ahh look what he's doing, he's chewing my hand off." It all seems like great fun, eh? But really what they're doing is telling that dog that it's fun to bite. They're breaking a taboo.

"He's only a puppy, he can't do much damage." Not yet.

Six weeks on

Six weeks down the road, the puppy's now three months old. It's a lot bigger. Its teeth are changing. If it's a big breed, the dog's going to be significantly larger and stronger. The things you did to him at six weeks old aren't as cute and attractive now.

You're no longer prepared to go to the dog. You want *him* to come to *you*.

You don't feed him first any more, because you suddenly want to show him that *you're* the leader now. In fact, you don't do a lot of things you used to do when he was littler and cuter. You don't want him to play bite or jump on you and do stuff like that.

The poor old puppy looks at you and tries to say, "Listen, you just programmed me over the last six weeks about what to do for the rest of my life. You let me get away with things like jumping up, play-biting, demanding your attention, getting picked up, being fed first. I thought I was the preordained leader. What's going on now?" You and that pup are now in a state of conflict.

If, at three months, you're not so sure about how cute the dog really is, by six months and nine months, you don't think the things he does are funny at all. And it's *not* funny when that dog's jumping up on your bed and attacking you in the morning, like he did when he was smaller, when you used to let him play with you in bed, fighting and growling around the place.

And there aren't any laughs any more when he comes in filthy dirty and jumps up on your couch because he was allowed to do it as a puppy. It's not funny now that he paws you like you taught him to. It's not funny that the dog ignores you when you call him. He's just sitting there thinking, "But you always came to *me*."

What the dog's trying to tell you is, "That first six weeks to three months was my learning window and that's what I learned. Now you want me to suddenly change all this? I like things the way they were. I'm not going to change. Now you're really going to have to challenge me to take it off me."

That pup's been set up for failure. The pounds are full of dogs that age. They're just like human teenagers, starting to explore and do things and consolidating their position from what they learned before.

Starting off on the right foot

It's a very long and hard road bringing a puppy back from that stage of disillusionment and confusion. It has to be a constant effort. Most people haven't got the time, or the will. In our disposable society, people find it easier to get rid of anything that doesn't meet their expectations.

Christ! Don't get rid of the dog. Get rid of the problem.

House rules

When you first take delivery of a puppy, it is okay to allow it to stay inside, but only for the first couple of weeks. And it should always be restricted when it's inside.

If you give a puppy free range around the house, it learns to scent-mark its territory for when it's older. The puppy automatically believes you've given it the right to do that. We all know that if it tries something like that when it's older, it's bound to be kicked out of the house. So don't let it traipse around when it's small.

I don't see you

When you first get your puppy, don't pay attention to it all the time. By looking at it, picking it up, you're giving it all the wrong signals.

Try treating the pup as if it's the lowest ranking person in the office or on the job. In the workplace you wouldn't see a labourer telling a foreman what to do, or an office manager coming along to the light globe changer and asking, "What'll we do now?" It's not snobbery. It just wouldn't work. You have to have your chain of command so everything goes smoothly. So the first thing is to pretend the puppy's not there most of the time, eh?

Every time you look at your puppy it thinks you want something from it, so it's most likely to come to you, even if it's a good puppy. I'm not talking yet about a dominating puppy. Dogs call each other by looking at each other. You often see people spend a lot of time looking at the puppies. When one comes over, they say, "I didn't call you. Go away, you silly puppy." But the puppy's saying, "Yeah, you did, you idiot. You looked at me and in my world, that means you want something from me."

This whole process involves things like feeding the puppy last, paying attention to the puppy last, giving the puppy the least desirable bed. Picture your puppy when it's an adult dog and how you'd like it to behave, then act and treat it accordingly. You'll ensure your pup a smooth transition right through its life by proving to it, "We are the leaders and you are the follower. We're never going to do things with you as a puppy that we don't want to do with you as an adult dog. That way, you're going to be round us for a while, eh?"

Easy does it

So if you want to ensure that you're not going to one day be forced to get rid of your dog, never play bite games with it when it's a puppy. If you do, all you're doing is teaching it to bite.

Don't play tug o' war with it. You often see kids playing it with a bit of rope or a towel or something with a dog. There's usually lots of screaming and squealing. It all seems like fun but what it means to the dog is that the child sounds like a frightened rabbit. To the pup, a tug o' war game is a contest over something that the pack's killed.

"I want it more than you, so I'm gonna nip you and get it off you." See where it's leading?

Tug o' war games, jump up games and bite me games with puppies aren't going to be attractive when the puppies are older and will most likely eventually lead to them being put down.

Freedom's just another word ...

People constantly let their puppies run free: "It's only a puppy, what can he do?" Do you want a list?

It can be killed by a car, get eaten by another dog, pick up a bit of bait. Anything could happen. But more than that, it's learning to be a free roamer.

"Aww, but he's a bit young yet. I can't put the lead on him because he really freaks out and it really frightens him." Rubbish. The dog just doesn't want the lead on him. He can't use aggression yet, so what he's doing is massaging your fears, tugging your heart strings. Don't believe people who say their puppy doesn't like that lead around his neck or he doesn't like that collar.

It might be a bit different with a choke chain. That will pull a dog's hair when he yanks on the chain, and that *hurts*. Any command given using a choke chain, the dog has a bad association with. But any collar's fine, so don't believe for a minute that the dog's "frightened out of its life" having a collar around its throat. That's a joke. The dog just doesn't want it.

A lot of dogs learn to avoid ever being on a lead because the one thing they remember from their puppy days is the reaction they received to the best show they ever staged — freaking out whenever they were put on a lead. Being under control doesn't traumatise dogs or puppies. By always making sure your puppy is secured in its own room or pen with its own basket, you're ensuring its safety and peace of mind, simply because it can't get away and roam around.

The puppy will adapt so quickly, you wouldn't believe.

I want my mum

If the puppy doesn't adapt as quickly as your timetable would like it to, it may start exercising its vocal chords the first few times you secure it in a safe, restricted area for the night. As hard as it may be — ignore him.

If he's whimpering turn on some soft music in the place you've left him. Before you close the door, leave the puppy a rag or a jumper with your smell on it. You can even put a little clock there very deep in its basket. The ticking of the clock's very similar to Mother's heartbeat. The puppy will lie down quite happily. It's got the smell of you. To all intents and purposes you're there.

If you react by going down to reassure the puppy or scold it or punish it, you're playing right into its paws. That's what the puppy wants. It wants you to come to it. Even if you get so frustrated that you hit the puppy, it won't be deterred. It'll learn to accept hits. It still wants the attention more than it minds the hits.

The best thing to do is, turn the radio up a bit ... nice soft taped music. Music soothes everyone and everything. If the dog has that little clock or rag of yours and there's nice soft music playing, you can freely ignore it. The whimpering will end. The pup was only doing it to see what it could get away with and how soft and gullible you were.

That's why dogs bark. "Woof woof. Is there a reaction anywhere? No? I won't keep it up, then. There's no point." The only time they *do* keep it up is when they get some kind of reaction. It's like barking at echoes. They hear a sound coming back, think another dog's responding to them, and go off.

Don't give in because they're pulling your heart stings. Imagine how you'll feel when they're pulling him out of the bag after he's been gassed because he's uncontrollable. If you go and spend time with your puppy every time it demands or cries, it's going to learn that's how it gets attention. That dog will scourge you for the rest of its life.

Is this a puddle I see before me?

To most people, puppies and piddle go together like bacon and eggs. But the problem and its solution has little to do with lack of hygiene on the pup's part.

Like so many dog problems, you need to know how a dog thinks to solve it. It's all about the need to restrict a dog's sense of freedom. If a pup's allowed to travel around the house at will, it feels it must put its own mark down.

But at first it's just involuntary movements. The puppy simply pees because it thinks it's time to pee. Once it understands where it's allowed to pee and what the restrictions are — where it's not allowed to go — it won't go anywhere near it and it won't piddle there. You're removing the problem.

Don't let your dog roam free around the house as a pup. You must keep a puppy restricted at all times in the house and any good puppy should be spending most of its day outside. If you have it inside all the time as a pup, it's going to want to be inside all the time when it's big.

Another problem of the peeing is that when a pup smells its own pee, it thinks, "This is all *my* territory. Because I'm allowed to run around as I like, it must be." So, while at first piddling inside might be an involuntary thing, eventually the dog starts thinking it's a leader and as such, is going to have to mark its territory.

That's why you get adult dogs peeing inside. It's a dominance thing, eh? They're trying to say, "This is my home. I don't smell anyone else's pee in this lounge and this bedroom, only mine. The only place I can smell anyone else's is the toilet, so that must be theirs."

You must give the dog definite signals. "This is *not* your territory. You provide the least amount to this pack every day. We're keeping you restricted after mealtimes and the minute I see your nose going down to the ground I can pick you up, take you outside and go to the toilet." Or, "After I feed you, I'm putting you outside."

Better still, feed the puppy outside.

While we're on the subject ...

Banishing a pup outside for sanitary purposes doesn't end with just showing him the back door. It requires a bit more on your part as leader. For instance, it'll make things a lot easier in getting the message across, if, when he puts his nose down to go to the toilet outside, and goes, you give him a tiny bit of cheese or something as a reward and say, "Toilet. Good dog."

He'll know what you mean. Dog's can't resist cheese. That dog will quickly learn that there's only one place he can use as a toilet. Because you have to restrict his activities outside, as well. Reserve a place for him to use as a toilet and enforce it. Put a little fence around it if you need to. No one wants their dog shitting all over the back yard.

So pick his place when he's a pup. You feed him in a separate area. When you see his nose going down, take him off to the side of that area.

Don't put the dog in exactly the same area to poo as where you feed him, because dogs don't do that, eh? When he's bigger he'll know exactly that that's where he eats and that other area's where he goes to the toilet. And nowhere else.

Out and about

So, apart from those couple of early weeks when your puppy may require a bit, but not too much, attention inside, you have to get used to the idea that a dog is basically an outside animal. You have to avoid any confusion and mixed messages right from the start. For instance, once you get into the habit of feeding your puppy inside, the dog expects it when it grows up. It feels it has the right to eat with everyone else in the pack, including the leader. You can't allow that. It *has* to be fed outside.

To be honest, I'm not looking at this at all from the human perspective. I'm saying it entirely for the dog's sake. If you don't do it right from the beginning, the dog certainly has a legitimate gripe. "Hey, you used to feed me inside all the time, what's the shit now?"

Don't even try to justify your action. Just make sure that, from the earliest opportunity, you always feed your dog outside. In fact, make sure the dog spends most of the day outside.

If the pup comes inside he must be put on his little lead. So that he can't annoy you all the time. You'll all be happier as a result.

Is this the puppy for me?

Because every pack, and every litter, is made up of differing individuals, there's never going to be a single approach that'll work for all puppies. Because those early months are so important in terms of letting a pup know where he stands in a pack and cementing the idea that *you're* really the Top Dog in his little mind, you need to approach each pup according to his individual personality.

Just remember that none of this stuff is based on human psychology. It's based on how each dog's brain works within the context of its pack and the dog world in general.

Fearful puppies

In every litter in every pack of dogs there are winners and losers. Invariably the puppies that win are the confident puppies. Puppies that lose are the little ones, the shy ones, the fearful ones.

Nature never rewards fear except where it prompts a creature to flee or freeze as a defence measure. That sort of fear can aid survival, but constant fear can't. So fearful pups are losers in their own world. But not necessarily in the human one.

Some people like a shy and crying dog. They hold a puppy and say, "Aww, Jesus, the poor little thing is so frightened. We should take it, eh?" In the dog world, a pup that's shy and retiring won't approach anything that has been claimed by another pup. It won't go for food first. It won't wander freely around the den, because it'll be attacked by all and sundry. It learns to stay in one place, where it's safe.

Any human who sees a puppy like that, almost always wants to take him home — just because he's so fearful looking. They feel sorry for him. There's some instant bond. "We love you already. Don't be frightened of us. We won't harm you. We want to protect you." They try to smother the puppy with love.

When they get the puppy home, they put him down, call, "Here puppy", and it runs off into the corner. "Aww, Jesus. Pull him back over here. He's so scared. Don't worry, puppy. We'll make you more confident."

Someone goes over and tries to pull the puppy back. The puppy nips them. "Jesus! Maybe he's not so fearful at all. Or maybe it's just fearful aggression."

Then, in a sterner voice, "Enough of this, puppy. You're going to learn to be sociable and you're going to lose all this fear."

Give us a break. Give the dog a break. All they've done is exacerbated the puppy's fear. By forcing all that attention on him, by pulling him out of his safe corner of refuge and making him interact with all the other pack members, the only thing the humans are saying is, "We don't understand your signals."

And those signals are pretty full-on and important from the pup's point of view. "I'm afraid. I don't know how to communicate. What you need to do is give me space to understand what's going on around me. After a while I'll come out of my own accord, but only when I'm sure you'll all ignore me. Stop looking at me. Stop trying to make friends with me. Stop trying to be all lovey-dovey with me all the time on this instant basis. I don't understand why you're doing all this stuff."

And you couldn't blame it, eh? To that pup, hugging, crowding and being picked up are too much like play-fighting. Back with the pack, it was always running last in the brawling. It was always the one getting bitten. So what that puppy's trying to get across is, "You just take a few steps backwards. When I'm ready I'll come out. When I work out who's what and where in the pack, things'll work a lot better for me.

"But you're not listening. I'm giving you signals. I'm constantly looking away. I'm never looking at anyone. I'm blinking my eyes and my head's dropped down. But all you're thinking is that I'm shy.

"Every time I give you a signal, you want to drag me over to you. I know what *that* means. Now I'm more frightened than ever. I know all that buddy-buddy crap doesn't work. Every time I tried it in the litter, it nearly got me murdered.

"It's even worse because you don't understand me. And you're supposed to be my new leader? For all I know you're going to attack me at any time and kill me. Now I'm even more afraid than ever."

Then there's those other contradictory messages. Remember that a leader goes to nobody. Every pack member comes to him or her. So the very fact that you went to the pup in the first place to pull him out of the corner was another conflicting statement.

While you're scaring the living daylights out of the pup, it also suspects that, because of the unwanted attention you're giving it, that you expect too much of it in terms of its standing in its new pack. Shit! You may even want it to be leader. It might be fearful and young, but it knows it doesn't have any of the necessary skills for *that*. With it as leader, the whole pack would be doomed. It's even more scared and confused.

In short, the more you try to force confidence on a fearful pup, the more frightened it will become — and the biting resulting from its fear could occur more often. You create an animal that could grow up to be a totally schizophrenic dog. And it will continue to bite out of fear. They don't mean to. They just react to the first time they met human beings when they had to bite because their signals weren't being understood. That was a very valuable lesson for that pup and it will more than likely remember that all its life.

Give me room

All you have to do with the fearful pup — and I guess it applies with any puppy, for all that — is to give it room to adjust and move. Let him have his own space and tease him out with little tidbits of food later on so he'll come over to you.

Recognise that a fearful pup does require special attention, but only in the sense that you don't give him too much. Don't look at him all the time. Don't bend over him. He'll only think you're trying to attack him.

Give him time to pluck up the courage to face everyone. Wait for him to make the decision. Don't force it.

When he does come out, only do things to encourage him. Don't make any fast, sudden or excited movements. He'll gradually work out that you're relaxed and unhassled. No staring at him. No play-fighting. He won't feel it's about to be attacked. He'll feel more secure. He will grow more confident.

Like everything else, it's all a matter of consolidating your leadership — not in a human way with hugging, talking, carrying the pup around and spending a lot of time with it. You just have to act like a real Top Dog.

The fearful dog in essence needs time. You need to give it everything in accordance with how it sees itself, not how you want to see it; not where you want it to be, but where it actually is. Because if that dog doesn't believe that you know where it's at, it's in total confusion.

It might be hard, but with all puppies, the best thing you can do is ignore them. People spend so much time on dogs when they're puppies, yet when they're older, the interest falls off. Why should people condition them falsely like that? It's a total contradiction, getting the puppy used to things they eventually won't be allowed to do. It's no wonder that when the penny drops, they don't like it and turmoil ensues.

You see, another facet of the fearful puppy is that it can eventually use its fear, or a reasonable facsimile of it, to get its own way when it grows up. It learns that humans can be easily conned. If it's in trouble, the once-was-a-fearful-puppy-but-is-now-a-conniving-dog can bung on quite an act. "Ohhh. Don't hit me. I'm soooooooooo afraid."

It mightn't be, but the performance is convincing enough to get all your old sympathetic juices working, and you back down. Instead of punishing it, you weaken and bring it inside. Sucked in! Bang goes your credibility as a leader.

The first law of puppy control is to start as you mean to go on.

Stroppy little buggers

The opposite to the fearful puppy has got to be the aggressive one. It's the litter mate that made the shy one's life hell long before you did.

In the pack, the mother has the ideal solution to deal with aggression. She ensures *she's* always more dominant. "Cool it. I'm onto you for everything. Get out of line and I've got your arse. That's the only way you'll learn." If a puppy loses every time, it ceases challenging.

Say one of her aggressive puppies bites her pads too hard during play. The mother doesn't muck around. A la *Crocodile*

Dundee, she says, "You reckon *that's* a bite? *This* is a bite." And she bites really hard. That's how they do it in the dog world. Violent? Well, that's a question I'll take up again shortly.

But really, a human's best weapon against an aggressive puppy is to be aloof. Don't lower yourself to its level. "Nipping me? I won't lower myself to bite a little shit like you back. I'll go and get some curry powder and put it on my hands. See how much you like nipping my hands then."

The happy excitable puppy

Every class has a clown. Humans always fall for it. If someone's out front making a dickhead of themselves, people invariably flock to join in. When a pup's the class clown, it knows it's happened upon a really handy tactic for getting people to do whatever it wants.

When somebody asks you to do something, you just act the idiot and they go, "Stupid dog. He doesn't know what's going on, eh?" The dog grins to itself. "Like hell I don't. When I was a puppy I learned that if I act the fool whenever you ask me to do something, I get to do my own thing." And it'll use that giddiness and excitement to get its own way when it's older.

Don't fall into its trap. Don't let it make the rules. Don't engage the puppy as it wants to be engaged. Its real mother would quickly bite down an excitable pup. "Do you really think I'm going to put up with that sort of behaviour around me? Get back in your place."

For an excited puppy, every time he gets worked up, I just go into a flat position on the ground. It spoils the act. "Hey! I'm putting on a show and you're not watching?"

"I'm not watching because I'm the leader and I'm not *supposed* to be watching. You're supposed to be watching me, not me watching you."

The puppies who do that aren't just acting the clown. They're trying to get you to pay attention to them and you're falling for it. When you do, you're not just pandering to their ego, you're recognising *them* as the leader. They're very smart — but a true Top Dog just has to be smarter.

The hard option

In all of this, we've been pussyfooting around a very important issue. If we admit that our human world is often too soppy and sooky for people to assert leadership over dogs and we recognise that in their world, violence has a real place, just where does it rank in the sort of things we're trying to do in reconciling our two worlds?

People can't really be trusted to use violence. When they do, they use it too well. It becomes a panacea for everything. In the dog world, punishment has its place but people have to learn the parameters of punishment.

A lot of people don't know a dog has an attention span of only four seconds. If you're going to punish a puppy for something, you better make sure it's within four seconds. Any later and the puppy believes you're punishing it for something completely different. That causes confusion. In an aggressive dog it causes more aggression. In a fearful dog it causes more fear and in an excited dog, more excitedness. "I'll just keep doing it that way."

Even by treating a puppy by forgetting the human side of it — forgetting about all the cuddles and how cute it is — involves you in some real political games. Fearful, excitable or aggressive, they're all capable of using their little quirks in their favour for the rest of their lives. So, you have to ask yourself, are you going to be there twenty-four hours a day to deal with them? Or would it be better to remove the problem?

In a real pack, the mother can afford to use the aggression because she's with the puppies all the time. You're not. Dogs will quickly learn they can do what they like when you're not around.

It's no good coming home, finding out what's happened and going off your head. "Look what you did while I was away, you bastard. I'm going to kill you." Because of the four-second time limit, there's no validity in it at all.

Humans have a larger brain. They're supposed to be civilised and constantly preach on how evil violence is. So why are they the ones who arbitrarily and consistently use violence against dogs?

People like violence too much. To dogs it's only a mechanism to survive. So forget the idea that you can beat aggression out of an aggressive pup or dog. Forget that you can calm an excitable puppy by becoming more excited yourself. And forget about making a fearful puppy more confident in ten seconds. They're all human concepts. They don't work with dogs. They avoid all the leadership issues I've been talking about.

Start as you mean to go on.

chapter 5

the seasons of the dogs

Of course your responsibility to your pack doesn't begin and end with the puppy years. For a start they won't really be years. Depending on the size of the dog, they eventually become the canine equivalent of teenagers. Little dogs can get there in five months. They seem to mature a lot quicker.

Bigger dogs retain that air of stupidity for two years or so. It doesn't matter how long it takes. They eventually *do* become teenagers and they're not all that different from human teenagers — remembering, of course, that they're *never* human. They're irresponsible, bold and naughty. But there's always a reason for it. For instance, when they start chewing everything in sight, it might be because they're teething. But those sorts of things aside, if you didn't establish your leadership and the pack rules when the dog was a pup, by three months of age, any boisterous behaviour will be well and truly entrenched.

Bundles of energy

What we call teenage dogs have just *got* to let go of their excess energy. When they do and they create chaos, it's no use screaming, hitting them and calling them juvenile delinquents. Your efforts are better served giving them the opportunity to use up that energy in a way that doesn't scourge you. You certainly *have* to find the time to make sure the young dog gets a good run, both in the morning and when you come home from work. People forget that this "teenage" period is really when your dog needs the most attention. It's also the age when most dogs end up in the pound!

Like human teenagers, the young dog will also be constantly testing you. It's at the age when it *really* feels the need to challenge your leadership. It'll be doing that all the time in the games it plays with you.

Armed with the knowledge of what could happen if you don't, you have to be prepared to always meet those challenges. You have to double your efforts to curb bad behaviour by the tricks of ignoring the dog, the loss of food and the loss of attention.

So many people blame the dog. "He eats off my plate, he sleeps in my bed and now the bastard ignores me. He just follows his own agenda." And on that basis, most of the dogs that end up on death row are of the teenage variety, simply because they've disappointed their owners.

You must never admit defeat to your dog. It's up to you to make sure it knows what your rules are. You're saying, "This is how you are going to behave from now until the day you die!"

The bitch is back

On that business of all dogs not being the same, females do tend to be more submissive, but don't be fooled. If you don't do your fair share of leadership, that word "bitch" can really take on its human meaning when they mature. Females have the ability to be what I call "passively dominant". Don't let them get away with it when they're young.

It's the same with little dogs. If they're allowed to get away with being snappy when they're young, they'll think that fear and violence are the answers to everything and become even worse when they're older.

Nowhere to run, no place to hide

A lot depends on how young dogs were treated as puppies and how they reacted with each other in the litter. A submissive pup that hasn't anywhere to retreat to can suffer through being constantly badgered by its more dominant brothers and sisters.

The other day I was outside a pet store where a whole lot of eight-week-old puppies were kept in a cage — all very cute for the people passing by. There was one submissive pup that didn't have anywhere to hide from a really aggressive one. It was giving all the signals: "Look, I know I'm inferior to you. I'm *not* challenging you. I just want to be left alone." But the signals didn't do any good. The dominant pup was still able to badger it. Whoever bought that submissive, scared pup was in for some major problems.

So, too, will the person who takes on the aggressive, dominant pup that's been allowed to get away with all that stuff. Both dogs will be well and truly screwed up. And they'll both probably end up in the pound.

There should be a law against keeping pups caged like that, where there's no sanctuary from all the noise, strange sights and smells and aggressive behaviour from other pups.

Many people believe they can burn off a young dog's energy by encouraging it to play boisterous and noisy games in the back yard. Then, when it's really excited, it's put back on its lead and just left there. So it starts barking. Barking in the back yard can quickly transform into barking in the pound.

If your kids are playing out the back, distract the dog by keeping it on its run with a nice bone it can turn its attention to. When you want to burn off youthful energy, take him away to a park or somewhere, where he can bark his head off without annoying anyone.

Above all, never revert to violence. A whack means nothing to a dog. "Hey! It's like a pat, isn't it — only heavier." He probably thinks it's fun. The thing is, he also thinks big whacks and other forms of violence are acceptable, even fun: "You just wait until I become a big feller, I'll know what to do."

Never darken my doorstep

When they're mature, dogs simply like being around you. The best punishment if it's misbehaving becomes banishment. One time I was called in by a woman whose whole family was being dominated by a Chihuahua they'd elevated to a position in their pack way above its station.

What was needed was a short, sharp shock. It came in the form of banishment to the worst commercial kennel we could find — where the comfort was spartan and the food as basic as possible (without being cruel). When that dog came back into the pack, it just knew it wasn't the leader. It didn't have to risk a challenge.

After an experience like that, a dog that was once a problem can become the most wonderful dog in the world, doing exactly what you say. After banishment, you start again with a clean slate. You've said, "Because of your behaviour, you're no longer welcome here. Goodbye!" When that dog is allowed home again, he's trying to tell you, "Please take me back. The food in that joint was shit, man."

When you have to go to such extremes, you can really play it to the hilt. When the dog's being driven away to his "gaol" state very clearly, "You're *banished*!" He'll remember the word later. He won't know the dictionary meaning of it, but he'll recall the sound, the tone of your voice and what happened after you used it. And he'll think twice before mucking up again. I've even thrown eggs at the car as the dog's been driven off, just to reinforce the message!

While the dog is away the family should learn all the rules to become good leaders.

The twilight years

As a dog gets on in years it loses its enthusiasm for playing, jumping or even climbing up onto your bed. If it does so, it does it very quietly. In other words, older dogs slow down.

The leader has to be a bit more patient in these circumstances. Don't be so demanding. Cold becomes a problem. The old joints'll seize up. Some breeds, like kelpies, can maintain their energy levels longer than others, but generally, dogs five to seven years old will take more time to do what they normally do.

Sometimes your kids, who've grown up with the dog and have always known him to be playful, will still try to keep him energetic. Remind them that he *is* getting old. He's more likely to sustain an injury. Don't expect kids to work it out for themselves. Unless you explain it, they won't know the signals the dog might be giving out.

The canned stuff

Maybe this is the time to talk about feeding your dog. I don't like commercial dog foods. They're just a mixture of grains, offal and chemicals. As far as I can work out, those chemicals are nothing more than speed. A diet of nothing but commercial pet food is bad enough for any dog, but with older ones, it takes a lot longer for their metabolism to break down the food. And the speed content is the last thing they need. They need less energy, not more. I think tinned and dry dog food are just like fast food. Bad for you.

Old and grumpy

As the years progress, some dogs do start getting aggressive. Sheepdogs are especially prone to becoming really cranky, mainly because they can no longer work at the levels they were used to and they get very bored. Dogs in that state will nip more. They'll generally be less tolerant and will want to spend a lot more time by themselves. Once again, explain the situation to the kids.

One of the worst things you can do is introduce a new dog into the pack, thinking it'll spark up the old feller. Old dogs simply don't like younger dogs. "The little bastard'll scourge me all my days!"

The dog will react aggressively, simply because it's protecting itself. We wouldn't expect Grandpa to go out to rave parties with our sixteen year old, eh? The old dog's teeth, eyes and hearing are all packing it in. It's natural defence system is actually winding down. He's got every reason to feel toey. The confidence he had at five years has been eroded. He needs calming. He needs reassurance, especially from his leader.

As an aside, you might notice your older dog reverting to puppy behaviour. That's the canine version of dementia. At this time, the old dog appreciates a hand. Don't hesitate to allow him inside more often. You might need to actually bring him in to the house and physically put him on his mat.

People don't always act like they should to older dogs. They refuse to admit to themselves that their old mate is getting on. It's almost as though if they lose the image of their dog at three years of age, they will lose the image of themselves. They sense their own mortality.

The final curtain

It's up to the leader to ensure a graceful and dignified conclusion to their pack member's life. It's at this time you can afford to relent a bit and bring in a few human considerations. Just remember, your dog still won't understand your concept of love, but it will understand kindness.

You can afford to let it get away with things you couldn't let it get away with when it was younger. You can still attempt the occasional game, but don't overdo it. Remember that stress means death at this stage of a dog's life. Give it an easy life. "You've served me well. Here's your super fund."

Be glad to do it for the last couple of years of your dog's life. It's not a matter of relinquishing your leadership and acting submissively. You're being a good and kind leader. Your dog understands that.

My own dog Jack can't walk as far as he did when he was a new dog, so I'm not going to make him. He prefers to go walking with Leanne. He thinks she's his missus. She takes him on a nice gentle walk to the park with its nice soft grass. He loves it.

All an old dog needs is no fast movements, no loud noises and good shelter. Even Jack's starting to get paranoid if there's too much excitement or noise.

If you have to leave the old dog alone, still refrain from making him feel as though you're frightened that something will happen. Don't sook. It will only disturb him. It might be the time to consider a mild herbal sedative to calm him down while you're away.

If it's for any length of time, make sure you leave him somewhere he's comfortable. Take him there beforehand. Get him used to the people, the smells, the sights and the sounds. Maybe drive past a few times before you actually board him out. It doesn't take much.

Lessening the blow

By rewarding your dog with kindness in his twilight years, you're actually helping yourself. It'll lessen the grief when he does go. And that day *will* come. Either the vet will point out that the dog's in pain or that its quality of life isn't the same any more. If you're lucky, the dog could just pass away of its own accord.

I remember one bloke who'd been annoyed by his dog's crying and whingeing for a couple of days. "I didn't have any time to look into it and he died. He fell down the stairs and died."

It should be wrong to feel guilty when your dog dies. After all, there *should* be plenty of good times together to remember. If you've got other dogs, they're not going to be upset. In the dog world, the natural reaction to a death in the pack is simply, "Jesus. I'm glad it wasn't me."

By all means, before you say that last goodbye, even though he's died, go out and have a final yarn with him about those good times. Take a bottle of something out there with you. Then bury him.

Then go out and get a new dog — a pup. Give another dog a chance to enjoy this world — this time, armed with the knowledge about how to do it right.

That's what your old dog would have wanted.

part 2

dogs behaving badly: the Dogman's problem-solver

Important!
Please, it's a good idea to get your vet to give your dog a regular check up. Some behaviour problems are caused by health problems.

chapter 6

personality quirks

You might wonder how I graduated from just being a dog to actually giving people advice on how to handle the multitude of problems they've created by not being prepared to pay attention to what the dog world's trying to tell them. Basically, it was by word of mouth. I was doing some voluntary work for the Animal Welfare League in NSW, when the word spread that I was actually making some sense. Funny that. People started recognising *my* signals.

Eventually I found myself dealing with people's problems on Fiona Wylie's radio show on the local ABC. Then I did a stint with Angela Catterns. Nowadays people ask me for help on the radio all over the place.

The problems I'm asked to deal with will be familiar with all dog owners, to a greater or lesser extent. Many of them will have sought answers before from all sorts of experts — academics, vets and dog psychologists. But the problems remain — because they haven't asked the dogs themselves, eh?

Stress management

I think my dog Pip's really stressed out. Can that really happen in the dog world? After all, it's a dog's life isn't it?

You can't get a more basic problem with your dog than stress. It's probably the biggest single cause of behaviour and misbehaviour that humans don't understand. And that lack of understanding on both sides is the actual cause of the problem.

For a start, dogs become stressed out because they don't understand people. They think you're living by their rules and you're not. You're living by the human rules and, as I've said time and time again, dogs will never be equipped to understand them. But they expect you, as the supposed leader to understand theirs. "What's going on? Sometimes you're the leader. Sometimes you're not. Sometimes you act all unnaturally towards me."

The symptoms of stress are many and varied. Stressed dogs lick themselves all the time. They'll pick one spot on their body and constantly lick it. Then there's excessive digging, or barking, or excitement. Maybe the dog's always on edge and perhaps it keeps showing aggression or fear at the same time.

There's also howling and wanting to be around you all the time. Stressed dogs shake nervously, blink their eyes a lot and constantly start at any noise. They also pant and yawn a lot.

The question of your ability as the leader, especially your ability to know and implement the rules of the dog world, is the root cause of every example of stress.

Mitch and Murphy are two little Jack Russell terriers. Their owner Jim constantly believes that if he gives everybody everything equally, the whole pack will run smoothly and everyone will have a great time. But more and more, Jim is finding that when he comes home, the dogs have been fighting. "I don't understand it. I give them everything. I share fifty-fifty between them. I've gone to a great effort to make sure we're all buddies and they seem to be ruining it for me."

Most of the time it's not out-and-out warfare. Murphy and Mitch jostle with each other for position. They growl threateningly. It's not so much, "Grrrrr! I hate you." It's more, "Outa the way. I get food first." And it's all to do with not knowing what their positions are in the pack. Neither wants to be the lower one, so they're always challenging.

Jim's clearly doing the wrong thing. The right thing would have been originally to have picked one of the dogs to be higher ranking than the other. If it were Murphy, he would always get his food first. He would always be recognised and greeted first, allowed through the door first, or awarded with a tidbit first. He'd have the prime sleeping area. All that would officially recognise that he was fitter for a better position in the pecking order than Mitch.

That's what all the bad behaviour by both dogs was all about. They'd been trying to give Jim clues about what he should do all along. Mitch wouldn't end up the loser. He'd be in a much better, less stressful situation. If Jim decided to make Murphy the Top Dog, all the brawling would end. Murphy would no longer have a need to bully Mitch. Murphy would go along with that. "Hey! I can stand up to Mitch every day and flog him. I don't want to, but if you keep putting him up as leader, that's what I'll have to keep doing."

Sort out who's to be acknowledged as the better dog and you'll never have a problem with that sort of stress ever again. Let's look at some other causes.

A dog that's constantly left alone will always stress out because it thinks it's no longer a member of the pack. Or it may think it's being punished for something and can't work out what it is.

You may well walk that dog and feed it, but if that's the only time you come into contact with it, it's really getting the very least of what it needs most — being around you. A lot of people think they don't need that interaction because they got their dog as a guard dog or a working dog. That's not fair. I know in my heart and soul that when a dog's kept outside and never allowed in to interact with other members of the pack, it feels it's being ostracised. And it doesn't know why! If your dog isn't allowed inside the house, just go and sit with your dog every day for an hour or so.

Not being consistent with your dog also stresses it out. "Don't jump up on me today dog, I've got my good strides on," will totally stress the dog out because it doesn't know why. The last time he did it you encouraged it and thought it was great. "Come on, boy! Up you jump!" This time he copped a whack in the head. That's stressful.

The idea that you can pick the rules and change them as you go along is no good for the dog. He's going to lose the plot.

People in the pack treating the dog differently adds to the problem. If one member of the family likes him jumping up, likes a bit of a wrestle and lots of hugging and someone else doesn't, the dog can't work it out. It's especially confusing if you, the leader, allow him to do something and a lower ranking member like one of the kids, objects.

It would be a really good idea if everyone in the family sat down and had a little conflab. "What's the best way of taking the stress out of Pip's life?" The best way is for you all to act the same way towards Pip.

Remember, Pip doesn't take tranquillisers or a beer to calm him down. His way is to eat away at himself or wander up and down that yard barking. He doesn't like doing that either, because stress makes him sick.

Conflict in the pack is another stress factor. If the humans are having a problem — some kind of family crisis — that drags on, the dog's often going to think that the pack's breaking up. In the dog world there wouldn't be that kind of stress because any conflict would be very brief, dealt with and forgotten straight away. In the human world people tend to keep things going for days.

the dogman

Of course when the dog starts signalling that he's stressed by odd behaviour, some of the aggression's turned to him. You whack him or scream at him. No wonder he thinks the pack's breaking up and no wonder he worries about what's going to happen to him when it does.

If you're arguing with each other, try not to do it in front of the dog and try to get it over and done with quickly. Hey! It'll do you good too because you won't be carrying all that bitterness and grudges around for long.

Kids are a classic cause of stress. Most people get a dog for their kids. They expect the kid to teach it, and the dog gets used to having its ears pulled and the child climbing all over it. But just like adult humans, dogs eventually get pissed off. If they kept pulling your hair and poking your eyes, wouldn't you? You'd quickly rouse at the child.

The only way the dog has of reprimanding children is to eventually give them a little nip. It will never happen without ample warning. As the leader and an adult, it's up to you to look out for and react to those warning signs. At first, the dog will try to get away. If it can't, it'll go into a corner, turn its head around and flash more signals — yawning, facing its bum to its tormentors and maybe rolling on its back — the ultimate submission signal. Poor old Pip will be trying to say, "There. Now you *have* to leave me alone because I've gone to the lowest position."

But the kids may only see that as an invitation to jump on the dog's belly. Of course Pip thinks he's going to get hurt. All his signals have been ignored. Now, out of sheer fear and desperation he turns around and nips the children.

And the dog always gets the blame. He also gets turfed outside, walloped, chained up or sent to the pound — for something that was never his fault. And you can't blame the kids. As pack leaders it's up to the adults to recognise the signals. And recognise the dog had no other way out. Its last resort involved using the only tools it was issued with to handle the situation —

its teeth. "Hey, you're the leader here but if you can't keep things under control, I will." And that's what you're considering sending him to the pound for. It's not fair.

Humans don't put up with their own kids for very long. I know because I've got three of them myself. "All right, kids. That's enough. Let's see what's on telly." Pip doesn't have a telly. He's only got his teeth. You can't expect your dog to take on the stress and boldness of your children if you won't do it yourself.

To prevent it occurring, all you have to do is constantly keep an eye on what's happening with the kids and your dog. And provide an area where your dog can have some form of refuge — where you can remove him from all that rowdy attention before things get out of hand.

"All right, kids. Pip's had enough. Let him go outside and have some afternoon tea."

If you're having your first child the dog will find all the sights and sounds of the new arrival very stressful. The first thing you should do, before Mum and baby come home from the hospital, is to tape-record the baby's crying. You can play it to the dog to help it acclimatise to the new changes. Do it at walk time and feed time so there's that good association.

Then bring home a wet nappy and dab around all the walls of the house with it. Believe it or not, the dog will think, "Hey, that little pup reached way up there to pee? It must be a real big dog, eh?" It doesn't matter how wide of the mark it is, what matters is the association the dog forms in its head. It will always look at that child and think, admiringly, "You're a bigger dog than me. I could never get up that high to pee." It also gives that smell of the baby in the house.

Don't get me wrong, despite the stress problems, kids and dogs *should* be together. You just have to ensure it remains a happy and safe relationship for both sides. God forbid there should ever be a day when children didn't have dogs because they got bitten because of your bad leadership.

Staying angry with your dog is another stress cause. My mate Danny had this bull mastiff called Hank, who loved digging holes. Danny had these kick bags and stuff and sometimes he'd come out and find Hank had ripped them all up. Danny'd get real angry with the dog and hit it. Then he'd have nothing to do with Hank for days. Every time he looked at the dog, he'd get really angry. Danny thought that was the way to show how pissed off he was. So for days he wouldn't walk Hank. He'd barely feed him and every time he saw him, he'd growl at him or scold him. He was doing completely the wrong thing.

I told him, "Your idea of staying angry with Hank is wrong. You should only have been angry with him for a few brief seconds. You should only have used physical punishment when you actually caught him in the act — not afterwards, because he wouldn't be able to associate it with what he did."

By prolonging the anger, Danny was making Hank think he was doing *everything* wrong. "Crikey! I try to do the right thing. I lie down away from my food. I don't bark. But I still get growled at. What's up? How does my leader *want* me to act?" He was totally confused. All he sensed was hostility and aggression.

Hank was a pretty big dog. Maybe he could have used his size and aggression to front Danny himself and say, "Okay let's have it out. This has been going on for too long. This is far too stressful. In my world it would have been resolved in two or three seconds and that would have been *it*."

How would he have done that? He would have forced the issue and attacked Danny, and probably ended up on death row. Mad dog attacks owner! "It just proves he was a bad dog." So much for justice.

What should happen in a case like this is for the owner to cut his anger short. By all means blow your stack, but be very brief. You're going for shock effect. You're not in a soap opera, you're in a two-minute drama. Anyway, once the anger's out, you'll feel better yourself and you can get on with things.

Moving house is stressful enough for people, let alone dogs. "Oh Jesus, where are we going to put all that stuff that's in the back room?"

"Better clean that up."

"Did we forget anything?"

"The kids are complaining about their new school already."

People can help overcome a lot of the stress by making it a bit of an adventure. But they tend to forget about their dog. He doesn't have the brain power for fantasy and imagination. He's spent years building up an association with the old place and the territory he once knew belonged to him, all the other animals and the people. Bang! Suddenly it's all gone.

The dog thinks you've been chased out. There's another pack coming in and it's going to kill you all. What else could it be? There's still plenty of food. So he's really stressed out. But whenever he seeks attention or assurance by his stupid behaviour or howling or barking, he's told, "Shut up! You don't even know what's going on. Can't you see how stressed we are, what with moving all this furniture and getting everything together? What would you know about stress?"

The dog looks up at you and tries to say, "Everything, because I don't know what's going on at all. I might as well be in the Twilight Zone."

Try to reassure him. Do lots of yawning. Don't hunt him out of the way or yell at him. When you get to the new place, take him out around the place early — on a lead, of course — so he can get used to the sights and smells. Keep him hungry so you can use morsels of food to encourage and reward him and help him make a new good association with what's going on. That way he's a lot less likely to become a howler or a barker in his new territory.

It's not a matter of socialising. That's you going to dinner parties and all that stuff. What you're saying to your dog is, "This is our new territory and this is everything in it."

Okay, so I've gone on a bit about stress, but I make no apologies for it. It's a very big thing in a dog's life.

My dog goes to the toilet indoors

There are a few different reasons why this happens. The dog could be afraid. There could be something wrong with its bowels. Or it could be dominant. Whatever the case, the solution is simple. Whenever your dog's inside from now on, put him on a lead. Tie him to your chair or any other object. But make sure the lead is short, about two feet. The dog can't go and pee or poo anywhere when it's tied on a lead like that. A dog that's tied up is in a submissive position because it knows it can't move around. Being tied up tells a dominant dog especially that it has no right to pee inside.

In Australia we're all likely to leave doors and things open in summer, so dogs that are normally kept outside can come in and make their mark without us knowing it. Don't hit them for it. They've made their own clear decision. You must then make yours. And that decision is to set aside an area outside to put them in when you have the doors open, or put them on a run.

What happens if you do catch your dog going to the toilet inside? Do you run up and rub its nose in it? Do you kick it? Do you scream at it? I wouldn't suggest any of those.

Don't rub its nose in it. It doesn't know what it is.

Don't kick it. It will associate violence with your leg and one day when you're playing football with it, you could get a nasty surprise.

Shouting's bad for it too. It's just you barking.

What you have to do is make a clear decision. Grab the dog by the neck, drag it outside and put it on a run or lead. That dog will never get off the run again when it wants to. You make the decision to bring it inside and when you do, you clip it onto its lead on its mat and it stays tied up.

That dog had been trying to take over and you've told it that it can't.

He's got nasty outside toilet habits, too

When Fifi wants to go to the toilet, she jumps off the verandah and, about two feet away, where you first step off, she does it. It's very annoying because my wife's ruined most of her good shoes.

Dogs should have a nice little fenced-in area in the yard that is consistently theirs — somewhere humans don't belong. They can do what they want in there. That's where we teach them to go to the toilet, because that's where they live.

Your main involvement is cleaning it out. It should be every day. But I'm a realist — you won't. But you'll need to clean it out every couple of days at least. It stops Fifi doing her business in your veggie patch, or where your lawn is, your beautiful flowers, or your wife's shoes.

Frighteners, loud noises and bottles of water are a lot of bullshit. Nobody's ever going to keep them up and people are going to laugh at you in the first place for trying them. When you establish the dog's own den area in the yard, the only time she moves out of it is when she's being walked or when she comes inside. In that area she can be a dog — she can chew, dig, sleep and poo. If she's outside and she puts her nose down, take her straight to her area.

Fifi now lives there. She has no choice. And that's the idea. You know what happens when you give a dog choice? It ends up in the pound.

My dog doesn't like children

My dog Bessie's a beautiful dog. To most people she's really great and she's really good around other dogs. The one thing she doesn't like is children. She seems afraid of them. Whenever they're around she becomes aggressive and wants to attack them.

Bessie has probably had a bad association with children somewhere in her life. We'll probably never know exactly what it was. You need to change Bessie's idea about children. The only way I know how to do that is to use food. In the dog world, food is like currency. Dogs will do anything for it — like humans will do anything for money.

It requires a bit of effort in this case. If there are kids in your neighborhood, arrange for them to help out. Take Bessie out for a walk on her lead. Arrange to have the kids placed along the road, playing or doing whatever it is they normally do.

Walk with Bessie towards them. As you go, slip Bessie a bit of cheese. Carry it in a bag, making sure she knows you're holding it. Bessie will really want that cheese because you didn't give her her dinner last night, eh? She's really hungry and attentive.

Every time you pass a kid, give Bessie a little piece of cheese and tell her what a great dog she is. Maybe down the road a bit, one of the kids is riding his bike. Get him to ring the bell. As soon as he does and you know Bessie's heard it, sling her another piece of cheese. She's loving this whole thing, because she really loves that cheese, eh?

By now you can slacken the lead off a bit. She's now looking at those children in a new light. I swear to God, you'll nearly see her tail wag when she spots them.

If you're not sure whether it's because of the cheese or the children, don't get too worked up about it — no one really knows, including Bessie. And it doesn't matter. It only matters that what you're doing is working. You only need to do all this for five to ten minutes at a time. Remember, Bessie's attention span isn't all that great.

Next day, you can change the routine a bit. Tee it up with the kids so that when you walk up to them with Bessie, get them all to give a nice big yawn. Then they hold a bit of food up, pretend to eat it, then throw it down on the ground *without even looking at Bessie*.

At this particular point, Bessie isn't ready for the kids to come up to her and make a fuss by patting her. It's all too early. But by doing what I just suggested, the kids'll be saying hello to her in a nice acceptable way — by giving her a bit of food. Maybe down the line they might all get much more friendlier, but for now, that's enough.

My dog won't leave me alone

My dog Cookie became attached to me very quickly. When he first refused to let me out of his sight, I thought it was pretty cool. But then I realised after about four weeks that he wanted to follow me everywhere — the shower, the toilet. He was like a shadow. But now he's a bit older, Cookie's starting to annoy me. Every time I leave him outside, he always ends up crying and whingeing.

Occasionally, the problem isn't antisocial behaviour, it's quite the other way around. To solve this problem, you're going to have to work from the inside out.

It's no good just putting Cookie outside and insisting that he cooperate. Doing that will shock him and he'll just keep up the complaining. Instead, you're going to totally ignore him — but in the dog way.

Whenever he looks at you, look away. If he comes to you, lift your chin up and turn your head away. Yawn, as though you don't even realise he's around.

If he becomes more adamant and comes to you and actually tries harder to get your attention, put your arms up high. You'll know it's working when Cookie gives up and walks away. Eventually he'll just lie down and begin to be a bit more independent.

There's a second stage ... Deliberately wander out of the room for a couple of minutes. Make it nice and casual. Don't pay any attention to the dog at all, even when you're leaving. If you make the mistake of sooking and saying, "I'll be back in a few minutes, so don't worry," the dog will misread your message and start worrying. Be sure of success by clipping your dog on a leash.

When you do finally stroll back in, stick to your guns. Don't do or say anything that might put out a message like, "Oh gee, did you miss me?" Slouch down in the chair. If the dog looks at you, yawn again. You're telling him, "No, I didn't do anything interesting."

That way the dog will soon learn that it's not missing anything while you're away. It will start getting used to the idea of being on its own. It will know that there's nothing to be frightened of. It's all right if the leader isn't around all the time. It may even twig that it's quite rewarding to have time to itself. Practise this for longer periods of time until Cookie is okay. Another dog would be a very good idea. It can be around all the time taking the attention away from you.

Hubba hubba

My dog Jock mounts my visitors' legs whenever they come over. What's going on?

It's most likely that your friends invariably give Jock preference over you when they arrive. They don't come and say hello to you first. They greet Jock. He, quite reasonably, believes they regard him as Top Dog. He's the leader. But when they turn their attention to you, he starts feeling a bit insecure. "Hey, I'm over here," he barks to remind them that they're committing a social indiscretion. So he humps the nearest human leg. It's his way of trying to dominate your guest.

To solve it, you've got to make sure Jock knows his place in the pack when visitors turn up. You'll have to rope them into your training program.

Let all your friends know that you want them to ignore Jock when they visit. Ask them to cooperate by yawning and acting indifferent if they make eye contact with him. Eventually he'll realise his true position in the pack and accept that he's *not* the leader.

Of course, Jock should always be on his lead when people arrive. If you feel the policy of ignoring him is working, you can let him off. But the moment he backslides, clip him back on.

My dog keeps tearing up the washing

My dog Mikey's out in the yard. I'm watching him through the window. He's tearing the washing off the clothesline. He's done this about a million times before. I've whacked him, I've tied him up but that seemed cruel. I tied him up on a rope, but he broke the rope and he went and did it again. I'm at my wit's end.

Well first of all, let's think what Mikey thinks about it. Is he getting enough exercise? Is he a bit bored in the yard? Maybe that's why he's gone out and thought, "Jesus, I've got nothing to play with. I haven't been for a walk. I haven't really been outside yet. Nobody's paid any attention to me. I'll go and get the washing. That'll do, I'll play with that."

It could be as well, of course, that if Mikey wants attention, he knows that washing's dear to you and that's going to get you out the door. There's many reasons why Mikey's doing it, but the solution's going to be pretty simple.

Put Mikey on a little run and clip him onto it on the days that you do your washing. On washing days it's On the Run Day for the dog. Remember that from now on, you're really going to have to keep your contract with your dog as far as exercise is concerned. You're going to *have* to give him a walk in the morning and you're going to *have* to give him a walk in the evening. Also, give Mikey a big raw bone on wash days. It's a fair reward for going on the run.

Give him something near his run that he can play with. Hang an old tyre or something from a piece of rope. He can jump at it. Maybe smear some nice old cooking oil from last night's roast on it.

Punishing Mikey for getting stuck into the washing won't work. It's much better that you ensure he's safely out of harm's way and still getting his maximum exercise. Organising a proper run gives him his own little washing line, eh? Remember, though, he's still going to need his regular walks. If you don't fulfil that part of the contract you'll end up with even more problems than you bargained for.

My dog's afraid of everything

I got my dog Seana from the pound, and at the pound we knew straight away that she was a very shy dog. She wouldn't even walk up to me, so I went over, bent down and was trying to be very nice and talked very soft, but she seemed to be more afraid. So I picked her up anyway, put her in the car and brought her home. For the first couple of weeks, I felt it best I spend a little extra time with her. She seemed a bit afraid about the new change and her new life. I decided to be around her a bit more to reassure her if anything happened. Of course things did happen — loud noises from the neighbours, cars and things like that. It made her even more afraid. She's even afraid of the washing machine when it's going round and round, and every time she shows that fear we do our best to go up to her and try to reassure her. "Don't worry, Seana. It's only the washing machine." But she seems even more afraid.

Of course she's more afraid. When you do that, Seana's thinking, "Oh Jesus, they're all scared too." She's even more unsure about who's going to protect you all now. There's no strong leader to protect her.

You really have to stop that cycle by a very simple method. Every time your dog shows fear, tape-record the sound — all the sounds you used to sook her over, all those sounds she's now terminally afraid of. What you're going to do is play them back to her gently. Play them when you're lying down beside her. Feed her tidbits so she's eventually going to gain a good association over a small length of time, with all those things that used to frighten her.

When you take her out for walks, don't always be bending down to her when she sees a strange dog or hears a car. Put your chest out more, tilt your head up like a real strong leader. "Come along, Seana. We're not afraid of this stuff. We're on a mission. We're going to keep on our way. We're not afraid of anything. I'm a good courageous leader. I know that you're a bit afraid, but I'm going to put a little extra courage in your meal tonight." Seana looks up and goes, "Oh my God, all my dreams have come true. Someone at least looks as though they know what they're doing."

Keep that confidence up whenever you go out together, when you're around other people and other dogs. Practice it all the time and you'll soon find that your shy, fearful dog was only staying that way because you'd been shy and fearful yourself and sooking her. Once you're acting like a true leader, your dog will mimic what you do.

One trick is to never actually *look* at something the dog's afraid of. Look over it, with your chin up in the air as if it doesn't even merit your attention. "That didn't frighten me. It doesn't even warrant my consideration." So if your dog's fearful but you maintain that confident style instead of being a sook, you'll have that problem killed.

My dog won't stop begging at the table

My little dog Harry seems to be begging at the table all the time — breakfast through to dinner — even if someone gets up for a snack in the middle of the night.

What Harry's thinking about here is, "The more you keep feeding me, the more I'll do it. I'll sit there with that sad, lonesome face and I'll jump up, scratch on your legs and do a happy trick. I'll do anything to get my tidbit."

Basically, you have to make Harry feel a very unwelcome guest at the dinner table. When it comes to mealtime, Harry has to be put in another room or put outside. Harry's going to be unhappy about this but this is where persistence comes in. If you're not going to be persistent about the food, how are you going to be persistent about anything else? Food is like money. You don't go sharing it with *anybody*.

So, from now on, Harry goes outside at mealtimes. Every time you walk past Harry with food, you absolutely ignore him even though he's sitting there with his little sad face demanding the food from you. The same if he's jumping up or crying. He's not asking you — he's *demanding*. He sees himself as the leader and is demanding food from everyone.

So everyone *has* to stick to the new rules — that Harry has to be taken outside, put on his lead and fed after people are eating. You're telling Harry, "The party's over. You're no longer gate-crashing any of our meals or snacks." It's going to be really good for Harry because it's going to prove to him that if he can't have food all the time, he's not on the same level as you.

As I said before, with this business about ignoring the dog, you're pretending he doesn't exist. "What dog? I didn't notice a dog?" If you keep that up when he's demanding and whingeing, it will stop him from begging. Ignoring him means absolutely no talking to him or looking at him. He will soon get the message.

My dog guards his toys

Bunji loves toys. I buy at least one a week for him and he has so many around his bed, I don't know how he gets in there to sleep. One day I thought, "By gee, I'd better clean up a few of these toys and make the poor little bloke a bit more comfortable." I went over to his bed and picked up one or two of his toys. Lo and behold, he bit me! I couldn't believe it. I put him outside. He growled all the way out and tried to nip me. I pushed him out the door and sat down thinking, "Jesus Christ, what went on there?"

Well, to Bunji, they're toys all right, but they're toys he thinks he's won. I bet every time you went out and bought him one, you came back and made a big fuss about it. "Oh Bunji, would you like this?"

Bunji thought, "Sure I'd like it. I'm going to get it off you. It'll be another trophy I've won off you, proving I'm higher ranking than you are."

Every time you brought a toy home for Bunji, he saw it as proof of his leadership. He even has his own trophy cabinet, only to you it just looks like the mess around his bed. To him, it's a display area showing how he won those trophies off you and you're not the leader any more. What you did was go in and try to steal his trophies. But he caught you! When he bit you, he was warning you off. He'd won them fair and square.

The first thing you need to do is take him out the back at dinnertime and feed him in a different place. While he's eating, go and get all his toys and get rid of them. Get a new bed and put it in a new place. Any memories of the old bed area might rekindle thoughts of his trophy-collecting glory days. You have to get rid of that concept altogether. Basically, anything that might remind him how he beat you in all those games has to go.

Are you still going to play games with Bunji? Of course you are. But from now on, those games are going to be games that you make sure you win every time. The best one is the ball game.

Before you play it, make sure he's hungry. Don't feed him for about a day and a half. Get some really nice liverwurst or other tidbit. Keep Bunji on a lead for the first couple of days. That way you'll keep control and stop yourself from being bitten if Bunji gets a bit stroppy.

Play a roll-the-ball game. Roll the ball. If he brings it back, give him a tidbit. Roll it again. Reward him again when he complies. When you're ready, you end the game. Remember, he's really hungry still. Show him a morsel of food. He'll really want it. He'll spit the ball out to get it — so flick it in one direction, and when Bunji races off to eat, pick up the ball with the other hand.

As a good leader, you're showing him you don't want any conflict in your games. You don't need to use violence. You just have to outsmart him. When he's off eating and you've got the ball, you've won the ball game.

Take that ball and put it up high somewhere. From now on, the only time you're going to play with that ball is when Bunji's hungry. You'll always get it back by giving him a little bit of food. Never leave any toy around for him ever again. They're dangerous because they make him think he's winning challenges against you.

My dog jumps up on everybody

Rajah loves jumping up on people. He does it no matter who they are. As soon as someone comes in the yard, or comes up to me in the street, Rajah's all over them. Why does he do it?

What Rajah's trying to do is put right a misconception. He thinks that every time someone comes up to talk to you, they're mistaking you as the leader. They don't realise that *he's* really the Top Dog. He thinks that by running up to them and grabbing their attention and coaxing a pat out of them, they'll show that they realise that he's really the leader.

The first thing you need to do is put him off the idea of jumping up in the yard. That's where most of it starts. Every time Rajah wants to jump on you for attention, simply fold your arms up high, lift your chin and turn away from him. In dog language that simply means, "Don't you dare jump up on me. I'm the leader. I'm the only one who's allowed to do any jumping up."

From now on, stop paying attention to Rajah all the time. You might think his stupid little antics are cute or funny but when you keep paying attention to him all the time, it makes him think he's the boss. That's why he's always jumping on other people. Only pay attention to him if there's something you want. Any other time when he comes up seeking attention, simply lift your chin in the air, turn your head away and yawn. That's the dogs' way of saying to Rajah, "No! I don't want any interaction with you at all." Once you've done it around the house for about a week, Rajah's been bombarded with the message that the only time he'll get attention in future is when you decide to give it to him.

That's the mark of a true leader. It doesn't notice anybody else. It doesn't ask anybody else's opinion. It doesn't pay any attention to anybody else.

Once you've established in Rajah's eyes that he's not the Top Dog, organise some friends to come over and take part. As soon as they arrive, tie Rajah up. When they go in, he can't jump up on them. Ask them to pay no attention to Rajah — to come straight in and talk to you. When they're leaving, throw a little bit of food to the dog. But don't say anything. The message will still be clear: "You're not the leader and you can't jump up on us."

After a couple of days, leave Rajah off the lead. If anyone comes by and Rajah tries to jump up on them, have them do as you did before — arms up high, chin up, head turned and yawn. Rajah will try it on everyone for a while but after about thirty seconds he'll get confused. He'll see everyone's acting like the Top Dog and not paying him any attention. He'll sit down. Call him over to you and get him to sit again. As soon as he does, say, "Good dog." And you, as the owner, can pat him. You've rewarded him for recognising your leadership.

Go inside but leave Rajah outside for a while. It's a little punishment, letting him know that he did the wrong thing by still trying to jump up. His leadership aspirations are over forever.

My dog's destructive when left alone

I try to do the right thing all the time by my dog Gypsy, especially in the morning when I'm going out. I try to give her everything she needs. I give her a few toys, I give her water and everything inside. I always thought she'd be safer and happier inside during the day. But when I come home, the whole place is destroyed. Clothes are torn all over the place, the couch is usually chewed, there's all sorts of stuff dragged around the room. Is the dog doing this because she's jealous of being left all day by herself or is it some weird kind of revenge?

It's *not* revenge or jealousy. One reason all that stuff could be happening is that Gypsy's afraid. Usually when dogs are anxious and afraid, they like to chew — mostly on things that smell strongly of you, and that's usually your socks, undies or shoes. I call it comfort chewing. The dog does it because it misses you and the chewing is nice and soothing for it. It gives the "virtual reality" of you being there.

If that's the case you really have to stop sooking the dog when you go in the morning, because really that's what's triggering it off. It makes every day a bad day for Gypsy. Try to act a bit more confident. Don't go bending over and saying, "It's all right, doggy. I'll be back later, don't worry about it." Because you're giving it a reason to worry.

If you've got an area in the house where you can put Gypsy where she *can't* destroy anything of value, please do. There must be somewhere — a laundry or the garage. The dog doesn't understand value at all. It's just the scent. The chair might just be something hard for her to chew on, or something different.

That covers the anxious side of it, but there's another possibility. The dog could be really bored. It hasn't had any exercise that morning or didn't go for a walk. If it doesn't get a walk and has to spend long hours inside the house during the day, it's very boring. The house is a very uninteresting place and there isn't anything much going on there.

It's the same as the clothesline syndrome — it's a way of getting something to happen. If Gypsy had had a walk that morning, sniffed around and had a bit of a play, she'd have something to remember. It's not jealousy or revenge — she's just finding something to chew because she's afraid or bored.

In regards to chewing — give the dog something to chew that she wants to chew. There are all sorts of things in the pet store you can pack food into and it's very hard to get out. If you have something like that, when you leave the dog alone it will have something to keep it occupied for an hour or two. By the time it's wrestled all the food out of it, it's tuckered out. Don't give the dog an old shoe or an old sock you don't need any more because she'll think all shoes are the same.

The problem often arises with little dogs, because people don't like to leave them outside. But a dog is a dog, no matter what size it is. It has to get used to being outside, even if it's one of those cute little fluffy things. If you can leave it outside in a run with a few juicy bones, it'll be fine. You can let it run about all day. For little dogs a properly fenced yard is ideal.

Be sure you keep up to that famous contract I was talking about if you put a dog in the run. Always give it two walks a day. It's a very important thing. If you don't you'll just transfer the problem you had inside to the outside.

My dog likes to dig up the garden

Every day I take my dog Jack out the back to be with me when I work in the garden. I like to dig, pull weeds, transplant and things like that. I put a lot of work into my garden. Invariably, if I go back in and come out again, he's dug up holes everywhere. I find he's done things like eaten the watering system I've just put it. He was with me when I did it. He saw how much work and care I put into it. He's seen how much time I've spent putting new plants in — and he does this to me. If I'm taking the time to do all this work, why can't he do the right thing by me?

Let's see how Jack sees this situation. He's a dog and the only thing he ever thinks of digging for is bones. And that's exactly what he thinks you're digging for. He thinks you've been out there all morning looking for a bone you've buried sometime in the past and still haven't found. When you go inside, he thinks you've given up, so he decides he's going to give it one more shot.

So he starts digging up that garden looking for that bone. He digs and he digs around the whole garden, but he doesn't find it either. When you come out, you see him standing there in the mess and you get very angry. But Jack's thinking, "All right, you've been digging for a bone. I've been digging for a bone, and neither of us has found it. What are you getting so angry about?"

The solution is simple. Now you understand what Jack thinks gardening is, it makes sense not to take him gardening with you any more. Separate him completely from your garden by creating his own little one. When it comes time for you to do your gardening, you can put him in his own little space that you've cordoned off. Make it the worst, grubbiest little place in the yard where you don't mind that he digs or makes a mess.

Bury some bones there from last night's dinner. So he'll be digging in his patch, biting and chewing, and you'll be in yours, digging and transplanting.

Interact with him still. "How are you going, Jack? Finding any bones?" You'll both be quite happy with each other's behaviour.

Just remember, Jack couldn't give a tinker's cuss about your precious garden, how highly you value it or how much work you do in it. You've got to put him in a position where he can't do something silly again. You've got yours, he's got his ... and never the twain shall meet.

My dog mucks up inside

Every time I let my dog Zipper inside when he's been out all day, he's into everything — he's up around the couch and he's onto the chairs and he's knocking all the vases over. He's broken more things than I care to remember. Half my precious stuff is gone and I still have that bloody dog and he's still doing the same thing.

Zipper obviously thinks he's a bit of a Top Dog. He can't understand why he's been left outside when all his underlings are inside. As soon as he gets inside he has to underline the fact that he is the leader. He does that by releasing his massive energy. He flies around the room, getting everyone to look at him. He's noticed. He's dominating everyone because they have to get out of his way when he comes flying through. Once everyone's noticed him, he lies down. Mission achieved.

This is a simple one. Call Zipper to you and put him on the lead. If, when you open the door, he tries to barge in front of you, simply close the door in his face. Do that a couple of times without looking at him and he'll become very wary about trying to race through the door ahead of you. When you walk through, call him to you. Remember, he's still on the lead. He can't rush because he's restrained.

Make sure you've got his little mat on the blind side of your chair, where you can tie him, because that's where he's going to stay now whenever he comes in. He's got no freedom now to fly around the room to convince everyone that he's really the Top Dog and he should have been inside all the time. You're not the ones on the lead, Zipper is. At the same time, he can't muck up and be shouted at and booted outside. He's safe. He still gets to come inside but he has his own little place. And having his own little place is a lot better than having to be got rid of.

He's bound to protest at first. He could well start barking a bit. The secret lies in two simple words: "*Leave it!*"

The key to using those words is how you say them. They have to be delivered in a real threatening manner — very authoritatively. It has to be low like a growl. "*Leave it!*"

Anyone can do it. The dog's already feeling threatened and submissive because it's on a lead when nobody else is. These words just confirm it. Zipper will quickly learn to lie down. When he does the right thing and is lying there, reward him with a little tidbit of cheese, a little scratch around the ear. That'll be reward enough. Zipper'll be getting what he wants, but he'll be getting it on your terms.

Coming inside is no longer a mad, stressful affair that ends in anger and violence, with Zipper being booted outside and you feeling guilty afterwards. From now on, Zipper will be lying peacefully beside your chair — and that's exactly the sort of dog you want inside.

My dog barks and scratches until I let him in

Paddy's a little terrier. When I put him outside to ... you know ... be a dog, pee and chew his bones or just leave me alone for a while, he gets most indignant. Give him about ten seconds outside and he's back at the door, scratching and whining. I try ignoring him. I try turning up the telly, but I just can't seem to override all that scratching and whining. The other night the neighbour rings up and says, "I don't mind your dog, he's a nice dog. But would you just shut him up and stop him scratching." So I go out. I hit him. And I come back in. I sit down. Twenty-five seconds later Paddy's at the door again and he's doing it all over again. I bring him inside, but I feel like a total loser. I reckon he's put it over me.

Well Paddy certainly feels like a winner. All that barking and scratching has got him inside. He doesn't care that he got a smack. "It's worked. I've got inside."

There are a few reasons why he wanted to come in. He might have been afraid. We've already look at handling fearful dogs. But if he's just pushy and demanding — and most of them are — have a bucket of cold icy water at the back door at all times. As soon as he starts scratching, demanding and whining, walk out and take him by the collar — don't say anything — and clip him up next to the back door.The moment he starts carrying on again, walk back outside, this time with the bucket of cold water and dump it all over him. As you dump it, say only "Cold Water!" in a loud voice and walk back inside. He'll quickly realise that every time he hears those words, "Cold water", and gets a drenching that he's in trouble for barking. He'll admit to himself that he's lost that particular battle and from then on he'll wait quietly outside until he's asked to come in.

When he does come in, clip him on his lead on his little mat to ensure that he doesn't muck up again and get booted out. Surely, as the leader you alone have the right to say who comes into the den and when. Being tied up inside isn't bad. It's you confirming your leadership.

My dog play-bites — and it hurts

When we play, my dog Major keeps biting me on the arms and shoulders. It hurts a lot. How can I stop him from doing it?

When he was a puppy, I bet you played games with him. When you rolled on the ground and you got him to attack your arms and bite you, and things like that, you would have thought, "This is all right. This is what pups do to each other, so we might as well keep it up." It seemed pretty natural. And it is. For dogs. Not for people.

You have to be seen as a leader. What you did wrong was get down to the pup's level and showed him it was fun to bite you. Of course Major went along with it. Dogs like to play-bite. But they don't do it for fun. They do it by exerting just enough pressure to signal to an opponent, "Okay, I'm stronger than you. I can hurt you more than you can hurt me. Therefore, without us going into a full fight, you just drop down below me."

At the age Major is now, he's testing you. Young adult dogs are always like that. Certainly you can't play about like that with Major any more. No more, "Let's wrestle." No more putting your hand into his mouth and encouraging him to pretend he's attacking you. Because he's really not playing at all.

What if he comes up and wants to play like that? And he will, because it's a game he feels he's always won. When he tries to jump up for another sparring session, fold your arms up really high and turn away from him. It's really strong body language, saying to the dog, "Bugger off! Don't you dare jump up on me. I'm a leader. I've suddenly woken up from my state of amnesia. You're a pup and you're not going to jump up on me any more. You're going to respect me as a leader.

"In future, when you come up to me, sit down. We're not playing games any more. I know now they're not games, that they're a challenge, and from now on I'm going to act to ensure that you never make that challenge again."

Make sure everyone else in the household does the same

thing. No one is to ever play-bite with Major ever again. It may be play-biting now but in future a child could get bitten and Major could end up in the pound. The whole family's going to have to realise that.

My dog doesn't like going to the vet

As soon as my dog Jilly goes near any vet, she wants to go right back out to the car again. It doesn't mater which vet it is. I've tried talking nice and calmly to her but it doesn't seem to work. In the surgery, she's so stressed out the vet invariably asks me to take her out for a while to see if she'll settle down.

The best thing is to start at playing the vet yourself at home. Put on a white coat when you take Jilly for a walk. Put on a white coat when you feed her. Wear it when you're around the dog, more times than not.

Get a little table like a vet's table. Lift Jilly onto it and reward her with little tidbits when she's on it. Get her used to it. Get her used to the coat. Feel the dog all over her body. Tell her how good she is — not in a weak voice like, "Oh, it's okay darling. It's all right Jilly, don't you worry." Use a confident voice. "Good girl, Jilly. You stand there. I have to have a look at you. Oh there's nothing wrong with you."

She'll be desensitised because you're doing all that vet stuff in the home. By the time Jilly gets to the real vet it won't be that much of a problem. You can even take your white coat and wear it when you're at the vet's, at least for the first few times. It's no big deal. You're play-acting and that's okay in the dog world. They love acting. Their whole world is based on bluff.

Jilly will make the association. You're both wearing white coats. The vet will start doing things to her that you've been doing. You can give her calming signals. Keep your chin nicely centred. Yawn. Speak in a confident voice when you encourage her. Always take a tidbit with you to calm her if it's needed.

I know a lot of dogs completely lose it at the vet's. If they're big dogs they can actually cause damage. People put muzzles on them and stuff. That can frighten the dog even more by promoting a fearful association. It might stop the vet being bitten, but it could cause side effects with the dog.

Finally, if none of this works, there are herbal sedatives you can use. This isn't a cop-out. There's nothing wrong with them. They just bring the dog down enough for it to think everything's cool.

Small things like walking past the vet's with confidence will eventually get the dog so used to the idea that she'll find the once fearful experience a bit on the boring side. At least she'll always leave there with confidence, rather than a bite of the vet's hand.

Help! My dog is getting old and cranky

I've had Jack, my old dog, for nearly ten years now and in all that time he's been nothing but a loyal friend to me. But lately I'm beginning to notice a change in him. He's a lot more short-tempered now and doesn't want to seem to want to play as many games. And the thing that's worrying me most, is that he's begun to growl at my children. Sometimes he even snaps at them.

Dogs, just like people, get a lot of problems as they get older, problems with their body and their mind. Their eyesight and hearing especially aren't as good any more. And their old bones and joints and teeth are beginning to get sore. The main reason that old dogs get aggressive is to defend their old bodies against a sudden jump up or push or young dogs or kids diving on them. Old dogs don't have any physiotherapists or doctors in their world — or so they believe. For them prevention is the only choice because as far as they can see there's no cure. Only death.

Old dogs can suffer from paranoia and dementia, so any kind of change in their life or a shock will do great damage to their mental well-being. Try to protect your old dog from these where possible. If you have to leave your old dog for a period of time the old dog should be with someone it knows, not a strange kennel.

If you're thinking of taking on another dog at this stage of your old dog's life, make sure it's either a six week old puppy so your old dog can get maximum controlling influence over it or another old dog, and make sure the new dog is of the opposite sex. Whatever you do don't get a pushy mature or a young, maturing dog of the same sex as these will *scourge* the life out of your poor old dog.

If you have young children, it is very important that they are *always* supervised around an old dog. Your old dog should be always provided with a Child-Free Zone in a separate fenced-in yard out the back. Now they can escape the child's scourging if they want without resorting to growls or nips.

Older kids should be set rules around the old dog. The main rule is: give our old dog peace and space. Don't force an old dog to do anything by pushing and pulling, and no more rough play or teasing.

After all, we wouldn't let the kids and teenagers dive all over, pull and drag and tease grandma and grandpa to death.

Help! My dog guards his food when I watch him eating

I've got a lovely dog called Fred and I love watching him eat up all his grub. The only thing is that he's started growling and snapping at me while he's eating. I was told to grab him by the jowls and shake him, but when I did this, he bit me as soon as I let go. I'm becoming afraid of my dog. Is there anything I can do other than putting him down?

Well, now you've had your say, let's allow Fred his say. In Freddy's world — the Dog World — staring at someone else means one thing: "I want to take that food off you." So when we watch him eat, Freddy is thinking, "Hey you! Don't you dare look in the direction of my food. This is mine and if I have to, I'll fight you for it."

So how do we deal with this?

Do not use any violence in this situation as this will only cause further violence. Instead, we're going to solve this by the

Dog Rules and using our superior human *brain* power. Always make sure your dog is first clipped on a leash before you feed him. Bring the food over, pretend to eat some, then drop the bowl down and walk away. Your job as Leader is done. It's as simple as that. Remember we're now in the Dog World.

Please don't leave food lying around all day as your dog does not need to snack all day long. Also when a dog controls his food like this, he begins to think he's much more important than he really is. Give your dog half an hour to eat his food, and if it's not eaten, distract your dog with a yummy bit of cheese. While he's chasing after the cheese you've just pretend-nibbled and tossed away, calmly take his food bowl away. The message you are now giving your dog is, "Eat your food quickly or I will take it back. I am the Leader here."

Help! My dog keeps jumping up on the bed

I have a little dog called Queenie and boy, she is a queen, hey? She sleeps on my bed every night and I find I'm getting gradually pushed towards the edge of the bed. When I try to reclaim my part of the bed she stubbornly holds her territory. Also when she wakes up in the morning, she barks and nips me until I get out of bed. But the funny thing about it is, she then just lies back down on the bed. I feel like I'm being kicked out of my own bed.

I've tried many things. I've tried throwing her off the bed but she starts nipping my hand. I went and got a slipper once to shoo her off the bed with it but she grabbed it and now she destroys them whenever she finds them.

What should I do?

We must first realize that this problem was caused by letting her up on the bed in the first place. Bed is seen as a very powerful place for any dog to rest or sleep.

You've mistakenly believed that you're Queenie's best friend, sharing everything, including the bed, fifty-fifty. But Queenie had another idea about this. She was thinking, "You let me up on the bed? That means I'm only one step away from pushing *you* off the bed, and as soon as I push you off the bed, then *I'm* going to be the true queen around here." But there can't be two queens in any household.

What you need to do is compromise. Don't throw Queenie out of the bedroom altogether and say, "You're now just a servant", because I think in this case it would be too hard on her and you.

Instead, we're going to get a little basket. We're going to tie a little leash so she can no longer get up on the bed when she's in her basket next to our bed. We're going to ignore all her protests and tantrums. If she's whining and crying about it, remember what she's saying, "Let me off this leash! Let me off immediately! I want to get back to my Queenie position!"

Don't give in to her demands. Ignore her. Don't look at her. When she sees you won't weaken she'll give in and accept the basket quietly. But it's up to you. For this to work, you've got to be *persistent* in order to win the day because remember, the only alternative to the basket in your bedroom is the dungeon — remember the Tower of London? — that's the laundry.

If you're persistent enough, this nice dog basket is where our little princess is going to be sleeping from now on. She's not going to be treated like a queen any more, and do you know what, she's not going to be called Queenie any more — henceforth it is decreed that she will be known as 'Princess'. I'm not kidding. By changing her name she will make a new association. She'll lose all the past ideas she's had about having far too many rights and privileges.

So we've got a nice compromise happening here. We've got a bed of our own. She's got a bed of her own. We're the Queen and she's the Princess. There's no need to get upset or for extreme measures to be taken.

My dog is forever bringing me back things

Mufti always wants me to throw things for him, so he's always turning up with new objects.

Jesus this can be annoying. Mufti could be doing it because he sees it as a way of getting a bit of extra exercise. Or he could be doing it because he sees it as a way of getting you to do things for him.

The basic, simple thing to do is ignore it. Every time he brings you back something, lift you chin up in the air, turn your head away and fold your arms. Make your body language say, "I do not want that. I don't want anything to do with it. I don't want you bringing it to me."

On the other hand, if you do want to play fetch with Mufti, it has to be on your terms. Get something special like a ball that you own. At the end of every day it goes back up on the shelf that you've picked. Use it to throw to Mufti every time *you* want him to run and bring something back. Anything else that's brought back is absolutely ignored.

Mufti will be forced to concentrate on the goodies he gets only when he brings back that ball. Those goodies are a little bit of cheese, or maybe a little bit of devon. Just make sure that at the end of the game, the dog brings you back the ball, you slip him a little bit of food and you take the ball. That ends the game. Say, "Game over."

That tells him that's the only toy you want him to play with and play is now terminated. I know there are persistent dogs that'll start jumping up on you and that. If the ignoring and the folding of the arms doesn't work, get a little citronella in a bottle. Whatever else the dog brings back, other than the ball, spray a little citronella on it and give it back to the dog.

The dog'll put it in its mouth, won't like the taste and will spit it out. I'll wager the dog will stop bringing you anything you don't want in future because it hates that taste so much. But don't let the dog see you actually spraying the citronella. Turn away to do it secretly and throw the stick on the ground.

My dog's afraid of thunder

I have a personal story about this one. I had this dog called Pokie. Jesus he was a big dog. He was a Rottweiler cross bull mastiff. We were great friends. The one thing that used to freak him out was thunder. When it started he'd be out barking and trying to bite the sky. It was kinda funny at first but he kept it up for hours and suddenly it wasn't funny.

I decided to tape the thunder and sicken Pokie with it. I started doing it at really low volumes when he was nice and calm and relaxed. I sat with him, acting cool and relaxed myself — yawning and feeding him little tidbits. Gradually I'd turn the volume up, continuing the confident body language and tidbits. I'd do it for two or three hours a day. Gradually Pokie started acting like me. Eventually, he became so familiar with the sound of thunder that he ignored it. It wasn't so much that he associated it with the nice morsels of food. He was sick of it. The body language and food had only relaxed him during the initial stages.

You can try the same thing with dogs that like a singalong and howl at thunder. There are other dogs that get really afraid. They run and hide under the couch or under the house and bark and howl. You try to coax them out and calm them. "That's all right, boy. It's only thunder." That frightens them even more because the tone of your voice makes the dog feel that you're scared too.

The best thing is, as soon as the weather forecast warns you or you see a storm coming, bring your dog inside. Let him hide under the couch. If it keeps him quiet it doesn't matter. Don't make a fuss and get down there with him and try to comfort him. Keep up your own relaxed demeanour. Patience is the order of the day. Don't be afraid for the dog, be prepared to actually help him. If you don't act and sound confident, it won't work.

This approach works with noises other than thunder. I went to see a dog one time and he was afraid of the tumble-dryer. Using the tape recording, the confidence and the food, in twenty-five minutes I had that dog asleep beside the tumble dryer.

My dog bails people up

Joe's this big-chested dog who likes strutting his stuff around the block. The problem is lately he's started bailing people up. He runs up to them, bumps them with his chest and sometimes barks really aggressively at them. I don't want it to turn into a situation where he bites someone. I'm also not sure if punishing Joe is the right thing.

More than likely, Joe thinks he owns the street. He's undoubtedly going out there and peeing to mark his territory. Other dogs recognise the signals. They're aware that he's claiming the street as his. The trouble is, Joe thinks humans can smell it too. He can't understand why people are still coming through his patch. Anything that passes by that doesn't recognise his signals, he feels he has to go to stage two and front them up. Thankfully he hasn't got to the bite stage yet.

By giving Joe such free access to the road and allowing him out the front, you're putting him on guard duty. He should really be out the back. He shouldn't be allowed to run free.

Even if he only goes out on a lead for his regular walk, he's still going to want to pee to freshen up his territory markings. If he ever jumps the fence, he'll still defend it. If he can't get out and he senses trespassers, he'll become a bloody nuisance by barking. The best solution is to keep Joe on a run at the back of your house. Then when you walk him, go somewhere like a local park where lots of dogs go to pee. It's neutral ground.

My dog chases anything that moves

We need to really sit down and talk about this seriously. It doesn't matter if you're renting a place, own your own home or have a small property, it's all the same. Your dog needs a yard where it can't get out. For the reasons I've outlined previously, that run should be out the back. It'll stop him chasing the cars in the suburbs, the chickens on the farm and the cattle on the land. In the extreme, if you can't afford to fence a yard you have to look at the second option, which is a run. Anyone can stick a few poles in the ground, lay some concrete and string up a bit of wire.

Chasing is a major cause of death among dogs. They get skittled by cars. They get shot by irate farmers. Chasing isn't good for them for other reasons. They go out of their territory. Before they know it they're on unfamiliar ground. They're confused. They're unconfident, and they're more likely to be killed, injured or get into trouble.

chapter 7

keeping it in the family

My dog's aggressive to me

Toby was always pretty pushy and liked getting his own way. I didn't really mind too much at first, but now he's openly growling at me and he nipped me the other day when I went near his stuff. I'm actually starting to be scared of him and I'm wondering what I should do.

This is a bad one. The first thing to do is to take him to the vet to make sure there's nothing medical creating his aggression. There can be no half measures dealing with this problem. You need to get rid of Toby. Send him off to a kennel for a week or two — preferably one of the most unpleasant kennels you can find, a real tough camp.

Tell whoever's running the place that you don't want your dog receiving any privileges whatsoever. Insist that he gets the bare minimum in terms of care, like just the bare essentials for at least a week.

In the dog world, any pack member who upsets the others, or resorts to violence unnecessarily, is booted out. He's gone too far — especially if he's challenged the leader like Toby's doing. *You* can't be expected to leave the den as a result of his misbehaviour, so out *he* goes, but just for a week. That will give you time to develop the rules by which he's going to have to recognise your authority and admit that you're Top Dog.

First, you'll have to organise to restrict Toby's movements. In future, whenever he's out in the back yard, you're going to clip him onto his lead. Do the same when he's inside. At mealtimes, he's to be fed last. In any activity, Toby gets attention last — and of all the family members, that attention's going to be less than that paid to anyone else. You have to reinforce in him the realisation that he's the bottom rung on the ladder. From now on.

See, in a real pack *nobody* gets tied up. Everyone's able to roam free. But not in *your* pack. Not in *his* pack. Not any more. His lowly position has to be cemented in his mind every day, from the moment he wakes to when he turns in. It might seem harsh, but at least you're not resorting to violence, like they would in Toby's wild world.

The strictness could be permanent. Toby must never feel like he's allowed to make an independent decision ever again. If he is, he'll revert to aggression. There's no doubt about that!

By avoiding violence yourself, you're actually introducing certainty and consistency into Toby's confused world. If he does come good, by all means relax a little and maybe let him off his lead — but if he mucks up, make sure he goes straight back on. At the same time, reward all submissive, obedient behaviour with pats, tidbits of food and encouraging words.

And if it doesn't work? Well, you'll really have to consider having him put down — especially if you have kids. The lives of a hundred dogs aren't worth the risk of one child being bitten.

My dog is jealous of my partner

I'm at home all day with my dog Hubert and I find when my husband comes home, Hubert starts getting very aggressive towards him. As soon as my husband comes home and gives me a hug, Hubert's down at his feet, trying to gnaw his work boots off. My husband's getting really annoyed at this behaviour and I'm afraid matters will come to a head and we'll have to get rid of Hubert. My husband has never been cruel to Hubert. He's always taken him for walks. I must admit, because he works longer hours now, he doesn't always get the opportunity but the thing is, he's always tried to be kind to Hubert. Hubert just doesn't seem to appreciate it.

What's Hubert thinking about this? Most likely Hubert's already manipulating *you*. Just for the exercise, I'll call you The Servant.

You're thinking, "Should I do special little things for Hubert during the day so we'll all get on better?" Hubert's got a better idea about it. He thinks the more The Servant does for him, the more he's got it over you.

When your husband comes home, Hubert looks at him and says, "You haven't been round all day. You don't know what's going on. I've been controlling things here all day. How dare you come over and grab my servant and give her a hug and a kiss and all that kind of stuff? You haven't even come over and said hello to me first.

"You're putting The Servant above me when I've had her in place all day. Bugger you! I'm going to start nipping at your ankles. You don't respect me as the leader as you should. You don't even walk me as much!"

The first thing you're going to have to do is recognise that by doing all those nice little things for Hubert during the day, you've been reinforcing his idea that you're The Servant. Don't do that any more. The dog has to be ignored for most of the time. It's going to have to spend a lot more time outside now. You're telling it, "You're not the leader, dog. It's me. I've reared children and a husband for fifteen or twenty years. You think you're going to put it over me? Forget it, dog. The game is up."

Hubert is quickly going to believe that now he's been toppled from his throne. He's no longer the leader. You're going to have much more freedom of movement. Spend it all on yourself — nice cups of coffee and so on.

From now on, spend short quality periods of time with your dog instead of all the time looking after him, seeing if he's all right. Pick a certain time — and that certain time's going to be when your husband comes home and when your children come home. That'll include everybody in having a good time. It won't be all, running to the dog.

The idea is to get the dog to do something for you first — sit down, lie down or wait — anything as simple as that as long as *you* have control. Don't pay attention to him if he comes running up to you, asking. That's him demanding to be the centre of attention. He's trying to divide you. Only pay attention to him when *you* want to. *You* call him over. You ask him to do something. When Hubert's done that, the whole family can pay attention to him for a brief period of time.

He's being told, "You're a valuable member of our pack. We *will* spend time with you but enough of this jealousy. It doesn't work. You're not the centre of our universe. We're all the centre of each other's universe — except that you're the bottom part of that universe."

It's a lifestyle change. It's not a party trick. None of what I say in this book is a party trick or a quick fix. You have to tell the dog every day in every possible way, "No, you're not the most preferred pack member." If you let him have his own way, you divide the whole household and cause a lot of anxiety and stress. The change has to be forever, it's as simple as that — and as simple as the dog will understand.

My dog thinks he's boss over my kids

We've had Bitzer for nearly five years. We had him before we had kids and I suppose we treated him like a child when he was a pup. When the kids came along, we didn't want him to feel left out so we tried treating everyone equally. We really thought everyone would get along better as a result. But now it doesn't seem to be working. I caught Bitzer growling at the kids the other day when they had a bit of food. We don't want to get rid of Bitzer. We really love him, but our kids come before him. Why can't he be like everybody else? Why does he always have to be the odd one out?

Bitzer knows he was around before the kids were. Remember, he also thinks of you as dogs and the kids as pups. In the dog world there's a definite pack ladder and Bitzer obviously thinks he has the right to be higher on that ladder than your kids. When he was growling at them, he was saying, "Get back, get down. Know your place. I'm always in front of you and I have the right to do anything I want to do first and take anything I want from you."

It's not really his fault because he can never understand the human side of the story. It's humans who are at fault here. You thought you could use the old human "fifty-fifty concept" with Bitzer and share everything. It doesn't work. Last time his response was a growl. Next time it could be a bite.

You have to make sure that the children always get everything first, before Bitzer. Start first thing in the morning. Who do you notice first? Your kids. Who do you feed first? Your kids.

When you come home from work and the kids run out to say hello and that dog comes racing out between them, bowling them over and trying to get to you first, don't let him jump up for a pat. If you do, you're acknowledging that he's more important than the children and you're rewarding him.

Another example of him believing he's their boss is in the games department. When the kids play ball with him, I bet every now and then, when they throw the ball, he doesn't let them have it back. To him, when he gets to keep the ball, he's won the game.

Dogs have a different idea about games. If they win, they're boss.

Food's another consideration. You can start adopting the principle that there's no more tidbits for Bitzer unless he does something for you first. That means the children, under supervision, get the dog to sit or lie down first. Then they pretend to eat that little tidbit before throwing it down to him. It clearly tells Bitzer that they're higher ranking than he is. "Yes we will share, but only a little bit after we've had ours first." It enforces the fact that you're the leaders and he's the follower. Leaders eat first. That's the golden rule of any dog pack.

There are things the kids need to be taught too — like, no more tug o' war games, or jump up and run around games, or hugging or diving on Bitzer when he's lying down. Bitzer sees all those things as a challenge. He'll readily accept it and a kid can easily end up being bitten.

Tell the kids that they're all going to have to learn to be calm around him — not play with sticks or throw stones. They shouldn't jump on the dog or wrestle with him. It will only cause trouble. Tell them if they want to keep the dog, they'll have to obey those rules, because if something happens, someone gets bitten, the dog will have to go.

A really good way of stopping the children being bowled over is to make sure that every time the dog goes near a child, it has to sit or lie down before it gets any kind of attention — a pat or a tidbit. It has to take a submissive position when it goes up to a child. It lets the child seem like a leader.

I know a lot of young kids like the dog to go into the bedroom and sleep with them. Mummy and Daddy usually think it's okay if the dog sleeps on the bed. But it's a dangerous thing to do because it puts the dog in the warmest and most comfortable part of the den. As I mentioned before, a dog understands nothing about sharing. You have to teach your kids that there's a new way of sharing. The dog needs a little bed of its own, down at the bottom of the kids' beds. And everyone sleeps in their own bed.

You don't have to put your dog outside. That alienates the kids from the dog. It's a good thing for a dog to sleep in a child's room, as long as it's on its own bed. That way it will know it's not as high ranking as that little boy or girl.

There'll always come a time when the dog's going to have had enough of the kids. Bitzer's going to start pushing them over, trying to get away from them or going over into a corner. And the kids are going to keep following. That's probably the most dangerous situation that can ever arise between a dog and a child. The dog has given all the signals that it's had enough: it's using its teeth, it's turning its head away, it's dropped its head. It doesn't want that child around any more. But the child doesn't understand. The next thing that happens is that dog will either bump the kid out of the way, or bite it. I don't expect kids to understand all the dog's signals, but the adults should.

When the dog gets up and walks away — and that's the simplest signal of all to understand — you *know* that the dog's had enough. That's what they do to each other. If young pups come around the mother when she's like that, she'll snap at them. You can't have Bitzer doing that with your children. When you see it happening, warn the kids and call them inside for a biscuit or something. That way the kids will find it easier to understand. *They* get the reward this time.

Even fence off an area of the back yard that you can secure as a sanctuary for the dog when he doesn't want human company. Inside it is a little mat that's only his. Inside the house the rules are the same. Nobody goes near the dog when it's on its mat. You can clip the dog on its lead when it's on its mat. That mat is now seen by everyone as a safety zone for Bitzer. The children know that whenever the dog's there, they don't go near him. He can't be annoyed and won't be forced to fall back on the only thing he knows that's right to do in those circumstances — simply nip the children to tell them to go away.

If your dog does not get the message and tries to go a step further like growling or nipping, use the Banishment Treatment I've already mentioned for about a week. That will clearly give him the message that he is not dominant over your children. Any more aggressive dominance, you will be banished again.

My dog's aggressive to my grandchildren

We have this beautiful little dog called Sheila. I must admit we spoil her a bit. The rest of the family thinks we treat her like a princess. Okay, so she gets to eat off the table, she gets to sleep on the bed. She even pushes me out of the way on the bed. She gets picked up and carried around. She's got toys everywhere. After hearing what you've said on the radio, I must admit she has the run of the house. But to be frank, we don't mind. She seems pretty happy and we all love the little tricks and things she does. The problem is that when our grandchildren come over, she behaves aggressively. When they arrive and come to get a hug or sit on the couch, Sheila runs up and pretends she's going to nip them and growls. She's very possessive of all her toys. The kids love Sheila, for all her nonsense, but I'm really afraid that one day she is going to bite them.

First of all, let's see what Sheila's thinking about all of this. She's the princess, remember? She has everything. The couch is hers. The toys are hers. Everything's hers, including you.

Then suddenly these two strange pups come in from another pack and they're getting all the attention. "They sit on *my* couch. They play with *my* toys. They get everything first. I don't think that's right. They don't live in my pack. I don't recognise them as part of it and therefore they shouldn't be getting any of that kind of attention. I should be getting it all first.

"Now they're playing with my toys. This is when I start getting aggressive. I'm drawing the line. They can't have my possessions. They're my trophies. I won them off Grandpa and Grandma fairly and squarely by showing them I was fitter, faster and smarter than they were. These newcomers have no right to take them. They're only pups."

When you get sick of how she's carrying on, she finds herself being picked up, put outside and shouted at. She thinks, "Now I'm being locked up. All my territory's been taken off me by those two. As soon as I get out of here, I'm going to show *them* a thing or two. They'll find out who's the real boss.

You need to be careful about a couple of things here. When you know the grandkids are coming over, clean up all the toys. To avoid becoming involved in an aggressive conflict with Sheila while that's going on, one of you take her out for a morning walk. Once all the toys are picked up, clean up around Sheila's bed (of course she's got her own bed, eh?) so that when she comes back, she can't find any of her treasures.

The next thing you're going to have to do is change your attitude to Sheila *forever*. Stop treating her like a princess. Stop carrying her around. Stop giving her food off the table. Stop paying attention to her all the time. Because *that's* what's causing Sheila to get into trouble with the grandchildren.

I'm sure that deep down, you *do* love your grandchildren a little bit more than you do her. But don't worry, you *can* have your cake and eat it too. You can have them over and you can get the dog to behave in the right manner.

The first thing you're going to organise is that when your grandkids come over, their dad takes Sheila for a good long walk. Ask him to play games with her and tire her out like you wouldn't believe. When she comes back, she's going to be so tired, she's going to want to lie down. She might be a little bit hungry as well. You've been cunning. At tea last night, you kept a special piece of steak for Sheila.

When she gets home from her marathon walk, keep her on her lead, take her out the back, and let her have a drink. When the children come out to see her, pretend to nibble at the morsel of food then throw it to Sheila. Hungry Sheila will have to lie down and eat that tidbit. Then she's going to need to digest it. Being tired, she's going to be only too happy to lie down and be left alone, because that's what dogs naturally do in that situation.

You then have the opportunity to have quality time with the whole family together without stressing over whether Sheila's feeling left out, or jealous, or aggressive. She's not going to feel any of those things because she's totally buggered, with a full belly.

Then, five or ten minutes before everyone's due to leave, bring her in and clip her lead beside your chair. Wise the children up first. They'll probably enjoy it. Ask them to ignore Sheila entirely. See that they don't come over to her at all. What they should do is yawn, act relaxed and pretend they have no interest in the dog. Everyone is to do likewise. No one's to look at Sheila. Just keep talking to each other as if she isn't there.

Sheila's not going to feel put out. Despite what you might think, she doesn't ever feel she has to add anything to human conversations. She really doesn't care that no one's paying any attention.

When it comes time for the kids to leave, bring out a special treat — a nice soft piece of cheese is great. Get everyone to go through the same charade. Pretend to eat their cheese and drop it down beside Sheila without even looking at it. All casual and nonchalant. Then the kids can give Grandma and Grandpa a kiss and take their leave.

After a while Sheila's thinking will change. "Gee, I love it when those little pups come over. I get a big walk, and when I come back, they've got a lovely tidbit for me and I'm getting to spend more and more time with them inside.

"I understand now that I don't have to challenge them. And Grandma and Grandpa have taught me that they're always the leaders of this pack and it's they who'll choose who's welcome in our den, not me!"

My dog gets pushy with visitors

My dog Sniffy is so pushy with visitors you wouldn't believe it. Sometimes I think she's telepathic. She seems to know someone's coming and she gets excited. As soon as the car pulls up, or somebody comes, there's Sniffy over straight away to make friends. She jumps up on their legs, barks and runs around. Of course everyone looks down at her. They pat her and they let her jump up, talk to her in squeaky voices, then she'll run away. She'll run over to us and try to do the same thing. But as soon as the visitors come inside, Sniffy won't leave them alone. She's all over them, jumping up to get a pat; seeing if they've got any tidbits. That used to be very cute when Sniffy was a pup but now we find it most annoying and wonder what the hell's going on in her head.

Basically what Sniffy is thinking is, "I've already got everyone *in* the house under my control. The next step is to control everyone who comes here." So as soon as visitors come, Sniffy runs out. People think, "Oh, let's say hello to the dog and go to her first." As soon as they've done that, they've told her, "We see you, Sniffy, as the leader. All those humans in the house there are below you."

When they go inside and Sniffy pesters everyone, Sniffy thinks you haven't remembered that she's the leader. "Oh, they might have forgotten in the last couple of minutes, I better go over there and reaffirm it." So she goes from person to person: "You think I'm the leader, don't you? You think I'm the leader? You think I'm the leader ..." So when everyone gave her a pat out in the yard and thought she'd just go away, they were actually giving her the okay to ride roughshod over all of you by recognising her as the leader.

The simple solution is to encourage all your friends, when they come to your home, to absolutely ignore Sniffy. They shouldn't object. After all, being scratched to death and harassed all the time isn't most people's cup of tea. To start with, though, they could forewarn you of their arrival. Get people to bip their horns when they're arriving, especially when they're arriving unannounced. Maybe you could put a sign out asking people to bip their horn.

When the dog hears the horn, produce a bit of food. Eventually Sniffy will come to you. Feed her and clip her on her lead. If she's off her lead when they arrive, they should hold their hands high and their chin in the air and walk straight through to the first human. They should try and reach that human before even making eye contact with Sniffy. That's why you hold your hands high. A dog can't see you. And when they can't see you, they can't gauge what you're about. In the dog world, a Top Dog putting his paw up and down is telling the lesser dog not to jump up on them.

When they reach that first human (probably you), they should embrace them and greet them warmly. Then they purposely do the same with all the other people there. Maybe after a couple of minutes, they finally say hello to the dog.

If you want Sniffy inside with you — and for the life of me I can't think why, because Sniffy can't talk and add anything to the conversation — have her clipped on a little lead in there. This shows Sniffy she has to have manners and she can't go running about demanding attention from everybody inside. If you leave her outside, she might get a bit jealous of the visitors. But if Sniffy is inside and on her lead, she's got her cake and she can eat it.

While she's inside, don't look at her. Why should you? Obviously she can't talk and be part of things. But occasionally give her a little tidbit of food, making sure you pretend to eat it first. Let it drop so she can get it. That way, Sniffy thinks, "Well, I didn't dominate them. I didn't climb over them all the time. But it's still a good thing for me. I'm still inside and I still got a little bit of food at the end of it."

My dog is aggressive with visitors

Cujo is very aggressive when people come. If a car pulls up, he's out there growling and carrying on, trying to bite the tyres. When the people get out, he stands there growling and sometimes he even goes to nip one or two of them. We've tried tying him up, but that doesn't seem to solve the problem. He only seems to have become more aggressive. Should I have him put down or can we change his behaviour?

Well let's see what Cujo thinks about all this. Obviously he thinks he's the Top Dog. It is *he* who decides who comes to the house and it is *he* who tests who they are. So he puts on all this aggressive bluff, saying, "Look, I'm the true leader here. I didn't ask you to come. You wait there until I've sniffed you and decided who and what you are."

Of course, by the time he's done that, the people standing there are afraid because he's a big dog. Then the dog senses their fear, which causes it to even nip. "Ahh! So you're afraid of me, are you? There must be some reason for that. Maybe I'll give you a nip for being on my territory."

The more you try to pull him away, hit him and shout at him, the more aggressive he's going to become because he thinks, "Who are *you*, trying to pull me away from this situation? You're only an underling. I'm the one who decides who comes here. How *dare* you try to drive me away."

And then when you end up putting him on the lead, Cujo thinks, "The bastards are restricting me all together. These strangers have come in and I'm tied up. The first chance I get, when I get off, I'm going to savage one of them."

The first thing you *have* to do is become Top Dog over Cujo. I've covered that earlier. It's important that you understand all of that. It's the first brick you're going to stand on. As soon as you've established that — by including the dog spending more time on the lead or on the run in general circumstances (not just when visitors come over) — you're on your way. If you only do it when visitors come, the dog will associate that as a bad thing with them. That will only cause the aggression to continue.

Leave the dog on the lead for longer periods of time. Reward him with a bone whenever he goes on it. The message is clear: "You're the only one on the lead, so we must be higher ranking than you."

The second part of the solution is for the visitors to also appear more higher ranking than the dog. When they come over, they're not supposed to notice the dog. They're not supposed to go to it. Sometimes people give a dog a pat to say hello, but it's an absolute no-no. Cujo thinks they're going over to bite him. They have to pretend that dog doesn't exist. As soon as your guests go inside, throw the dog a juicier than juicy bone. He'll remember that and have a good association with the visitors.

Later on, you can probably bring the dog inside, but also have him tied to a chair. By then he's developed a good association with the people. The next few times they come, have the dog tied inside. They still shouldn't notice Cujo, but do lots of yawning, relaxing and blinking. Everybody should carry on as though the dog's a bit of the furniture. The dog won't feel threatened.

Just before the visitors are leaving, produce a nice bit of cheese. Like I've suggested before, pretend to eat a small bit of it and when you're passing, drop a bit down to the dog. The last thing that dog will remember of the visitors is, "They didn't annoy me while I was here. I got a nice bone when I didn't go up and hassle them. Everyone seemed nice and relaxed, so I was cool. Nobody tried to interact with me so I didn't get into trouble. And I got a nice tidbit when they left. Ahh, visitors! They're not too bad after all. I think I've changed my mind about them."

Remember, always make sure the dog's hungry when the visitors are due. When you know someone's coming round, don't feed the dog. Wait for your visitors to come so that nice juicy bone has its full effect — that's a double whammy.

My old dog hates my new dog

My old dog Jack met my new dog Buddy about five or six days ago. When he saw him for the first time, the hackles went up. I thought, "Jesus, what's going on here? What's up, Jack?" Then I looked over and saw Buddy cowering and looking really frightened. I sent Jack off to his place and tried to reassure Buddy. "Hey, don't get down like that. Jack didn't mean that. He's just getting grumpy in his old age." I started patting Buddy and every time I did, Jack just started to growl. It grew worse Now I worry that if I leave my two dogs alone, they're going to start fighting and one of them's going to get hurt.

The main problem began really when you started patting Buddy first. What you should have done was given Jack heaps more when you took Buddy home. If you'd given Jack tidbits of food at the same time, he would have thought all his Christmases had come at once. You would have been telling him, "You're my number one

the dogman

dog, Jack, don't worry about that. I'm sure that other feller will fall into line when he realises he's at the bottom of the pack."

Being bottom of the pack isn't going to worry Buddy. He's going to think, "All right, if I don't get in Jack's way, if I don't take pats that he should get, if I don't take tidbits that Jack should get, if I stand well back and wait my turn, me and Jack are going to have a pretty good life between us."

So always remember to feed Jack first, but don't forget to tie both dogs up when they're eating. Otherwise Jack's likely to scoff his, then go over and terrorise Buddy.

There are a few other little things like that you need to remember. Don't leave bones and toys lying around. They might cause a challenge between Jack and Buddy. Buddy's going to end up being hurt. Even if he only goes to smell whatever it is, Jack will become aggressive and might bite him. That's why it's also a good idea to pick up all your kids' toys from the back yard. They're just as likely to spark a blue as a bone will.

Continuing the buttering up of Jack — always encourage him to have the better spot, a bit more comfortable, and Buddy's a bit less so. Buddy will understand, he knows the rules. Stuff like that will ensure Jack and Buddy get on fine. You're giving your dogs a clear signal and stating exactly who's higher ranking than whom in the leader's eyes. And that's the way things'll stay until one of those dogs dies.

My dog is aggressive to our neighbour

Buster's not too bad around most people. He does gets a bit excited sometimes. But most times he's all right and he'll accept a pat and that. But for some reason he doesn't like the bloke next door. Every time our neighbour goes to work, or comes home, Buster goes off and tries to get through the fence at him. I'm worried that our neighbour's going to put us in to the council.

Buster's obviously had a bad association with your neighbour. It mightn't be anything nasty at all. Maybe your neighbour only shooshed Buster out of his garden or something. Whatever it was, it doesn't matter. What *does* matter is that Buster's angry with him. The strategy here is to convert that anger into something good.

Once again, our tried and trusty ally in this is going to be the dog's food. From now on, only feed your dog when the neighbour's around — in his yard or just passing by. The food will distract Buster every time. He's always going to prefer eating to hassling the neighbour. Eventually, after being called to eat every time he spots the neighbour, he's going to eventually put two and two together. It's a good association.

You can try the same thing in relation to a walk. When the neighbour's around, call Buster for his walk. In the dog's mind, the neighbour's presence will seem to be the reason for another enjoyable walk.

If Buster hasn't completely alienated the man next door, you might try to enlist his help. When Buster's on his lead out the back, stroll over and start chatting with your neighbour. Try to look relaxed. Laugh a lot. Appear as though you're both having a really good time. To Buster that signifies that if the two pack leaders can get along together, he has to be friendly too.

On another day you might go for a walk with Buster on his lead along the adjoining fence. Tee the neighbour up to walk past on his side in the opposite direction. Act a bit. Yawn at each other. See if you can't get the neighbour to carry a morsel of food. When you meet, he can pretend he's eating it. He can look and sound as though he's really enjoying it.

Then, when you start chatting, he can toss it to Buster. Keep chatting while the dog scoffs it. That's a ripper of a message. Your neighbour's willing to share his food with Buster. That automatically makes him an extended member of your pack. You're saying to the dog, "Whatever ideas you had about our neighbour before, change them!"

And Buster will quickly change his attitude. I'm not saying they're going to automatically fall in love with each other or even that after a week, the neighbour will be able to come over and sit down and have a yarn with Buster. But you will have success.

My dog is aggressive to my neighbour's dog

My dog has taken a sudden and terrible dislike to my next-door neighbour's dog. In fact, the feeling's mutual. Sandy feels the same way about my Billy. I don't want to fall out with my neighbour, so how can we stop it?

I bet I know what's happened here. One day Billy's gone over and peed in Sandy's garden, or Sandy's come over and pooed in Billy's. As a result there's no clear line over whose territory belongs to whom. Both dog's are thinking, "I better keep an eye on that other bloke. He's trying to pinch a piece of my patch. If he's going to keep trying that, I'll go and grab a bit of his."

Or maybe someone's nipped in and taken a bone or some other treasure from one back yard to the other. Whoever lost their prized possession is thinking, "That's the last time I let that bludger in here. He's nicked my bone. I can smell it over at his place."

A fight has always been inevitable. Your job as leader is to ensure that everyone remembers there's no violence in your pack, for whatever reason, unless you condone it. And you're never going to do that, are you?

The violence those dogs are showing towards each other amounts to total disobedience. They're thinking they're the leaders and they've got the right to sanction violence. It's just not on. The reality is, they're fighting over something that doesn't belong to either one of them. It belongs to you. You're the leader.

Even though there's a successful solution, those two dogs are never going to be the best of buddies. What you have to do is define or redefine the rules by not allowing the dogs to trespass on each other's territory. For a start there has to be a clearly defined fence that marks the area where the dog isn't allowed. If your dog can jump the fence, then clip his lead onto a long wire staked at both ends. He can run up and down, or lie in sweet repose, but he mustn't be in view of the other dog. They can't be allowed to see each other.

Second, when you take your bloke for a walk, make sure he doesn't pee outside the neighbour's door or on the road in front of it. Then use the lure of food to help create a better atmosphere. See if you can get your neighbour to cooperate. Have both dogs on their leads on opposite sides of the fence. Make sure the dogs are hungry. When they see each other, feed them their tidbits. Every time they behave appropriately, each of you should reward them with a piece of food. Every time they muck up, admonish them — growl down on top of them. That's telling your dog, "I don't appreciate this behaviour." As soon as your dog lies down, reward it with another tidbit.

Like I said, it won't solve the rivalry completely. Any incident could trigger both dogs to start scrapping again. But at least you're gaining some control over the situation.

My dog hates my cat

This is a very complicated one, but again it's very simple. Dogs basically chase cats because cats run away from them. Ninety per cent of the dogs are just curious. They merely want to see what's in their territory. Ten per cent want to attack and kill the cat. We'll deal with them later.

For the curious majority, what I tend to do is keep the dog inside. Make sure it's hungry and have some nice food on hand. Have the dog tied on a short lead to the leg of your chair. Make sure all the human members of the pack are nice and relaxed and giving out non-aggressive signals.

Bring the cat in. The cat'll be smart enough to stay away from the dog. They're always very evasive when they first meet dogs. Whenever your dog looks at the cat, say those two words: "*Leave it*!"

The dog will turn its head away. Slip it a tidbit of food. This will help the dog understand that it's not rewarding to look at the cat, but it *is* rewarding to leave it alone.

If the cat's movements aren't been studied by the dog all the time, the cat won't be as toey. The dog will keep looking back at the humans in case there's a likelihood of another morsel of food. It's forming a good association. If someone slung you a few bucks every time you agreed not to look at something passing in the street, you'd be happy to go along, eh?

After a while the dog will feel a bit more confident around the cat. At that stage, as the leader, pick the cat up and sit down near the dog with it in your arms. Don't let them sniff each other or anything like that. Concentrate on trying to get the cat comfortable with the situation, because he's the one to work on now. You don't want the cat reacting every time the dog moves because the dog, in turn, will react to the cat's movements. Always let the cat make any moves, though. After a while, the cat will decide that the dog's no longer a threat and no longer reacts to its movements by running after it. They'll eventually get on fine.

For that ten per cent of dogs that just really want to kill that cat, it's time to make a big decision. Are you prepared to build a separate run for each animal so they won't meet? Because the two will never get on. The best thing to do is keep them separated. By all means, try the good association therapy I've suggested for the other 90 per cent, but with these other dogs, you can never be guaranteed of anything.

out and about

My dog is aggressive to people when I take her for a walk

Daisy and I love gong for a walk every afternoon. It's meant to do a lot of good for both of us. But as soon as we get outside, Daisy changes from this beautiful angel little dog into an aggressive little devil. She's all right with other dogs, it's just strange people. She doesn't seem to like them at all. She seems to want to go at them as though she's some kind of a seven foot tall monster dog, but she's only small. I try to pull her away and scold her but the more I do that, the worse she gets. She tried to bite my finger the other day when I was waving it at her telling her not to be so aggressive. I'm now getting frightened that it's all getting out of control.

Once again, we've got to work out what Daisy's thinking. She's probably had a bad association with a stranger somewhere down the line. Now she's extending that to every stranger she meets. After the first time it happened and you took her out for a walk, she probably immediately became aggressive. And I bet the moment she did, you tugged on the lead, tapped her on the nose and told her, "No! You're a bad dog! Don't do that!"

"Of course it's bad," says Daisy. "In fact it's twice bad. First because I became aggressive with that strange person and now because when I did, my owner attacked me as well." She's become totally confused — so much so that she decided she'll attack people long before you even know they're there. Sometimes that can mean she'll pretend she doesn't see them until the last minute. Then she can rush out and give them a really good nip. Many people try to alleviate the problem by keeping their dog on a lead and trying to get people to associate better with her. But that can only make the problem seem worse. Dogs like Daisy can become even more aggressive again.

The first step, as always, is safety first! Make sure Daisy is on her lead, then there are a few changes you can make when you're out with her. Whenever you see a strange person approaching, don't get all uptight yourself, tighten the lead and admonish Daisy. You're supposed to be trying to make it a good experience for her.

First of all, make sure that she's hungry before she goes on her daily walk. A hungry dog is a more obedient dog. And if Daisy gets tidbits every time she sees a stranger passing, she's going to start making a good association with strangers.

Remember to make the tidbit special. She's got to think it's all worth it. Also, see if you can get a few people together that the dog doesn't know. Arrange them strategically down the street.

Go out with her on that day, making sure she's hungry, but *don't* give her any tidbits. Ask the people to absolutely ignore Daisy and as you're passing, they should pretend to eat the tidbit and then drop it at Daisy's feet. Daisy will quickly put two and two together. "Jesus, why should I chase these people away? They drop food for me. They must be someone from my pack."

For your part, make sure that Daisy's on her lead at a safe distance (about one and a half metres), greet each stranger warmly with a cheery, "G'day". Yawn and act relaxed.

If you keep that up for a couple of days, the dog will feel more relaxed too. Occasionally the so-called strangers who are now seemingly friends, should throw tidbits to the dog themselves, after pretending it's something they're eating. The message will be, "There's no threat here. You're getting a food treat. The leaders seem to get on pretty well together."

Down the line a couple of months you won't need to keep Daisy away from you on the lead. It may only take a couple of weeks, but don't rush it, because it's important. Eventually, she'll be able to stand right there beside you with a stranger. They won't be exactly hugging each other — and I'll explain what that's all about later — but for now, what you've achieved together will be enough. Now you'll have no one attacking anybody else, and nobody afraid. Nobody pulling leads, being stressed out and reviving bad associations.

My dog is aggressive to other dogs when we go for a walk

Whenever we take Sasha for a walk and she sees another dog, the bristles go up and she does that stupid little cry as if to say, "Let me at that dog. I want to get it." I don't understand. Normally she's great with people but as soon as she sees another dog, that's it. It doesn't matter if she's off or on the lead. Not to be able to take her out would break both our hearts.

Actually, you could be a large part of the problem. Often, when people are out with their dogs and they see another dog coming towards them, they tense up and think, "Uh oh! Something's going to happen." They automatically tighten the lead. When that happens, a dog like Sasha looks up at you and thinks, "Are you frightened of that dog? Don't worry. I can chase that dog away if you want me to."

When you tighten the lead, Sasha reads it as confirmation of what you want her to do. "Yup, you're definitely afraid of that dog. I'm going to get rid of it." When the other dog responds in kind, it's on for young and old.

To stop Sasha being aggressive to other dogs, you're going to have to start acting more like the leader you're supposed to be. For a start always have her on a lead. That's the greatest form of control there is. Then stop acting like you're fearing the worst and start acting confidently — like you know what you're doing.

Put your chest out and your chin up. "I know there's a strange dog coming up the road, but I'm not even going to look at it. I'll pretend that it doesn't exist." Sasha will be looking up at you and thinking, "Jesus, you look like a confident dog. You've convinced me that dog isn't worth two bob. He's certainly not worth wasting my time on, then. He's no threat to us, eh?"

When Sasha looks up at you with admiration like that and doesn't go for the other dog, reward her with a little bit of food or a scratch behind the ear. You'll be saying, "Well done, you followed the right order." Remember to be persistent because success won't come overnight.

Whatever happens, don't hit Sasha because she'll make a bad association with that other dog and next time will be even more aggressive. And it may catch you by surprise, as she'll be a bit more cunning and wait until the last second before attacking — because she thinks that way she'll avoid being hit again.

My dog hates being tied up in public

Jerry loves going to the shops with me, but he hates being tied up when I'm in there shopping. I have to tie him up, because I don't want him hit by a car or something like that. The other day a terrible thing happened when Jerry was tied up. Someone came up, tried to pat him and got nipped. I'm afraid to take him to the shops any more because he might get into serious trouble.

When Jerry's tied up, the first thing he thinks is, "Jesus I'm tied up and I can't get away from here if anything happens. My leader's gone and left me. I don't know where she is. That means I'm on my own and anything can come up and attack me. I can't get away. I could be easily killed.

"When that dog came up the other day, I was just minding my own business. The next thing I knew he was wanting to touch me. I gave him all the signals telling him I didn't want him around. I was blinking my eyes, I was yawning, turning my head away. Then my hackles started going up and I dropped my head down, but still he kept coming up to me. He stared at me all the time and kept coming in a straight line like he wanted to fight me. The next thing his paw started coming towards, me and I thought he was going to aggressively dominate me. So I bit him. I tried to get away, but I couldn't. Fortunately he got the message and backed off."

Remember that Jerry thought that chappy was a dog because that's the way he thinks of all humans. The best solution to the problem would be for everyone to realise that they should never approach a dog that's tied up, because they all think like Jerry. They're afraid they're going to be attacked. When someone goes to pat the dog, they think they're going to be attacked and they take the last resort to protect themselves — they bite.

So please, if you see a dog tied up and you want to do it any kind of a service at all, yawn, look away and walk off. That way the dog will think, "Phew! At least they understood my signals and gave some back. Maybe I can relax my guard a bit whenever I'm on a lead in public."

In the meantime, until the public gets that message, you should try to desensitise your dog. You have to reduce the fears he has when he's out on the lead. You can do that by arranging for people you know to help out. When Jack's on the lead, they can walk past, giving consistent signals — yawning, blinking and turning their head away from him. Don't let them lean over and try to hug him, try to talk to him or pat him.

You should realise by now that some dogs only see those sorts of things as threatening. You hear stories where people say, "My dog didn't bite anyone for ten years. Then one day I took him out and he did it." It could happen at any time to the best dog or the worst dog.

My dog won't behave in the car

My dog Fred is a bloody nuisance in the car. He runs up and down all the time and I've nearly had five or six accidents already. I don't like tying him up because he looks so sad and I'm sure it spoils the whole trip for him. I don't really want to leave him at home.

Once again, you've got to look at what makes Fred tick. The reason he runs up and down in the back of the car is because when he sees other cars and people flashing past, he thinks, "Oh wow! Look at them move. They must be really afraid of me. Hang on. I'll give them an extra chase just to reaffirm that it is me who's making them run like that."

Well, you obviously can't arrange a co-driver and the dog certainly can't drive, so what you have to do is put Fred in the back in the lowest possible position on the floor. Tie him to the floor with about 30 to 60 centimetres of lead. It'll keep him from running up and down and prevent him becoming excited.

Sure, Fred's likely to protest and will bark really loudly to be let off. But don't give in. Especially, don't yell at him. He only thinks you're joining in his barking. Just turn up the radio louder. Maybe get a CD or tape with your favourite music and turn it up nice and loud. It won't worry you because you like it, eh? You won't be able to hear the dog barking and nor will Fred himself, so he's eventually going to give up.

You're telling the dog, "Hey, you're definitely *not* the co-driver in this particular limousine and besides, I'm keeping you nice and safe. If we have an accident, you're not going to whack me in the back of the head and get us all in trouble."

It might take a couple of days, but eventually Fred'll give up his rowdy behaviour. Whenever a dog hears loud noise, it "closes" its ears and puts its head close to the ground. It's as simple as that.

Play it safe and practice all this stuff first where there's no traffic around and you're not likely to cheese off your neighbours with your loud music.

My dog won't let me clip him on his lead

Dino has this inherent hatred of the lead. As soon as it comes out, he causes a big kerfuffle. He'll jump up and down. He'll even growl. Sometimes he's nipped me. He obviously doesn't like it but I know he needs it to protect him in case he runs out onto the road or gets into a fight or something.

Let's first consult Dino. He believes *you* should be on the lead, not *him*. He thinks he's the leader. "In all the other things we do during the day, I win the little ball games and all the jump up on the couch games — and suddenly you decide you're going to put me on a *lead*? I'm not having any of that. I'm the leader. If anything, *you* should be on the lead." He thinks, "Well bugger you! I'm going to do everything possible to stay off this lead."

Again, we're going to use a food to deal with this because it's the main motivation. Food will nearly always work because if you keep Dino hungry enough, he'll do anything for food. So carry a little bag of food with you and don't feed Dino before you go out. When it's time for him to come on the lead, pull a bit of that food out and throw it to where he is. He'll pick it up and eat it. At the same time, he'll be aware of exactly where the rest of that food is. Shake the bag. As soon as you do, Dino will be at your toes.

Order him to sit. Don't give him any more until he does sit. Once he's sitting calmly, clip him on his lead. If he decides not to sit, just turn away and hold the bag of food to yourself. He'll think, "Jesus, I've made him turn away and eat it all himself." When you turn around again he'll most likely be sitting.

When you're clipping on the lead, keep feeding the dog food. After a while, you can introduce the reward system and pay the dog when he sits calmly — about every fourth to fifth time. At all other times simply praise with "Good Boy".

My dog drags me on his lead

It doesn't matter if we're going to the shops or going for a walk, my dog Tank drags me everywhere. He just loves it. By the end of the walk my arms are so sore I don't know what to do. I've half a mind not to take him walking again.

It's a dominance thing. Tank thinks he has the right to drag you everywhere because it makes him feel as if he's in control of the walk. He's the stronger one. Obviously he thinks he's the leader. He wants to sniff everything first, pee on everything first, wants to be able to challenge everything first. It's quite normal. He chooses the speed of the walk, which is usually at a breakneck pace.

To be frank, he'd won his challenge probably before you even put the lead on him. I refer you back to the previous case study. But let's imagine that you've managed to get the lead on Tank and you've made it to the front gate. By then he's probably already dragging you in the direction he wants to go. At the gate, turn the tables on him.

"No. You've decided you want to go that way. I'm the leader. I've decided we'll go this way. I'm dragging you in the opposite direction." And every time you do that, turn around, look at him and say, "Back!" Bring your hand down hard, putting your palm clearly in front of his face, like an old-fashioned traffic cop's stop signal, and walk on.

If he tries to come out in front of you again, remember he's trying to make an independent decision once more. He's trying to make you look bad as the leader. Whip around and walk off in the opposite direction. When he starts catching up, put your hand in front of his face again. "Back!" You're telling the dog where you want him to be. That shows him that his plans to force himself ahead simply had him left behind. It requires persistence but you will win it.

Dogs don't like losing all the time. If they keep losing, I swear they get embarrassed. They usually sit down and scratch themselves because they're totally confused by losing so many times. Eventually they never want to try that challenge again.

Another way of stopping your dog from dragging you around is to let him get a head and shoulders ahead of you, then saying nothing, ignore him and change direction, walking straight into the dog's side. Keep going. Every time the dog pulls ahead, keep changing direction so you are walking straight through the dog. Your dog will quickly learn to stay back at your heel.

Another way a dog will try to take control over a walk is when they see another dog. They'll want to go over and say hello, or have a chat, or even challenge the newcomer. And they want to do it first. They want to do everything first.

Similarly, all through the walk, your dog will want to pee everywhere to mark its territory. That's another little thing they have to do first. In both cases, you have to assume control. When he lowers his head to pee, pull the lead and jack his head into the air. Do the same thing if he shows interest in another dog.

You *can* do it — even with a big dog. Loudly say, "Leave it! Leave it! Leave it!" as you annoyingly jerk their lead until they leave it. The dog will quickly learn that it is not allowed to scent mark.

As for greeting other people and other dogs: "You can forget about that too, Dog. I'm the one who'll decide who will socialise and who we're going to meet. And *I'm* the one who'll greet them first. If you attempt to socialise first, I will loudly and firmly tell you to "Leave it" and put my hand palm first in front of you to show you what I mean." Again, praise your dog when it does the right thing.

My dog chases everything, even when he's on a lead

We live in the suburbs and we always keep our dog on a lead when we go for a walk. But everything that passes by — a car, a person, even a leaf — he tries to chase it. He's nearly broken my hand a couple of times.

When you take him for a walk, make sure he's hungry. When you see an object that he wants to chase — a bird, a leaf, a car or a person — order him to "Leave it", as you place your hand in front of the dog's face like a traffic cop saying, "stop". As they pass, produce a nice morsel of food, hold it up to the eye. When the temptation is passing, repeat the order: "Leave it!" Once the person or whatever has passed, throw the food down at your dog's feet.

After a couple of weeks, maybe a month, your dog will have gotten out of their habit of chasing everything.

None of this is rocket science. It's simplicity. It's persistence, consistency and confidence.

sheer disobedience

My dog ignores me

It breaks my heart because I do everything for her. From the moment I open my eyes in the morning, I run straight to Cissy to see if she's all right, to make sure she's not cold or anything. Even before I have my shower, I fix her a bit of food. When I have breakfast, she doesn't seem to want her food, but she wants mine. I don't mind. I feed her a bit of bacon. Then when it comes for her to do something for me, she absolutely ignores me. I think, "Well, I do so much for you and you don't return the compliment."

the dogman

Basically, what Cissy is thinking is that because you're doing so much for her, she must be the leader. Because she wants to be a good leader, she's obeying the rules of the dog world and not taking notice of any of your demands. You have no right to make them.

You're just going to stop paying so much attention to Cissy. In fact, you're going to have to stop paying any attention to her at all. You must only feed her or walk her at certain set times — that *you* decide. Sometimes you'll just have to forget that she's around. That will tell Cissy that you've changed your attitude and decided that *you're* the leader. As such, in the time when you used to do everything for her, you're going to find time to do things for yourself.

The less time you start spending around her, the more things she'll decide to do for you. You're turning the tables. You're starting to ignore her. You'll only do things for her when you want something from her. Remember you are the Leader from now on. You should think, "What have you done for me lately?" instead of, "What can I do for you?"

My dog won't come on call

I've got a dog called Muffy and we love to go down to the park for a walk. The problem is, when I let him off the lead, he's gone and he won't come back. I can call him from here to Kingdom Come, but he still won't come back. I must admit I get so frustrated, I chase after him screaming, "Come back here you stupid dog. I'm going to kill you when I catch you." Muffy just looks back and I swear he laughs at me.

Muffy's not laughing at you. What he's really saying is, "Aha! So you're running around like me and barking, eh? You must be having a good time as well. That's no problem. You keep following me and I'll keep running around. Wheeee!"

I bet when he *does* come back — and I know he does, because it's part of his challenge to see what you'll do next — you hit him and say, "You come back faster next time."

Muffy thinks, "Oh yeah? If I come back I get hit, eh? I won't bother next time, thanks very much."

So what was supposed to be a nice walk has suddenly become this really aggressive episode, which nobody likes. What's most likely to happen next is that you decide you don't like taking Muffy for a walk. So he stays in the yard. More problems. Muffy ends up at the pound because he's bored and barks all the time.

What you can do is simple. You're going to take advantage of the dog's evening mealtime to get your message across. If necessary, change the evening routine so you can take the dog on a twenty or thirty minute walk on his lead. As you walk along, feed Muffy little tidbits. Vary the route. Walk in zigzags. Go up and down hills and backtrack. Muffy will follow because he's *starving* and he knows you've got the dinner.

Keep walking ahead of Muffy. Then change tack. Drop behind and call Muffy back. Keep offering the food. He'll soon get the message that when you call him, he receives a nice reward.

You can start the process in the back yard, but move further afield as you succeed. As you progress, graduate to a longer lead. Then let him off the lead. Muffy will quickly learn that when you call his name, a nice experience will follow. He's not going to be hit. He's going to be fed. It's a great example of you using your bigger brain over his pea-sized one.

Sometimes my dog won't bother bringing back the ball

My dog Sammy loves playing ball with me. I throw him the ball and he brings it back. But after four or five goes, he won't. He just sits there and chews on it. He comes back to me okay, he just won't bring the ball. If I try to fetch it, he picks it up and runs away. I look like a bloody fool.

Let's see what Sammy thinks about all that. He figures you're bringing out the ball for him and he thinks, "Right! Another challenge! We'll play a few times, make out we're neck to neck — nil-all at half time. As soon as the second half starts, I'm going to run away with that ball and not bring it back. Sometimes I'll drop it and go back to the owner, but that'll be just a fake thing. 'Is this what you want? D'you want me, eh?' But I know in my heart and soul that it's that trophy that you want. I'm so confident about leaving that ball there that I know that if you make a run for it, I can get back to it first, grab it and run away."

You see, it's not so much a game to him as it is a challenge. He's proving that if he keeps the ball at the end of the game, or if he grabs it if you go near it, he's fitter and faster and better than you. When he leaves the ball out there, he's showing off his trophy to the world. But when you go near it, of course he's going to grab it and run away. He thinks you're trying to steal it.

The solution? From now on, only play the ball game with Sammy when he's hungry. And you're going to have to do it permanently. Put him on a short lead and throw the ball. When he fetches it and comes back, give him a bit of food.

Throw it like that a few times so he'll associate the food with bringing back the ball. After a while, only give him the food once every five or six times. He'll still know the food's coming so he'll always bring the ball back. When he comes back, of course he's going to have to drop the ball to get the food. So throw the food in one direction and the ball in the other.

You haven't dragged the ball out of his mouth. You haven't had to fight over it. There's nothing bad associated with it. The only association is a fair trade-off. He wanted the food. You wanted the ball.

When you get the ball, do your own lap of honour around the back yard. "This is *my* trophy. I won it now, dog."

At the finish of all of that, take the ball inside and put it up somewhere special where he can't reach it. From then on, only bring it out when *you* want to play with it. That's how you'll win the ball game. That's how you'll keep on top of the dog.

Remember, when playing with your dog don't ever do it with sticks or something easy to find that the dog can get himself, like a plastic bottle — they'll scourge you. There's a million sticks and they'll keep coming back. The dog can always win that game because there's always another stick. If it's only the ball or some special toy that you show interest in, that will be the trophy that'll really matter.

when the bark's worse than the bite

My dog barks too much when left alone

Our neighbours have been complaining recently that our dog barks too much during the day when I'm at work. They reckon if it continues, we're going to have to get rid of him.

First, let's examine some of the reasons the dog might be barking. The most common one is that it's lonely. Simply, the best thing to do is to get it a companion. If you've got a male dog, get a female. If you've got a female, get a male. If you don't want to do that there are other things you can do.

You can leave it inside in the laundry with water, food and nice music on the radio. Make it loud enough to block out any outside sounds. That'll help mask the barking. If he hears the music inside and can't hear anything outside, he's got no comeback. There's no echo even, coming back from his bark. You see, if he's barking outside, there's often an echo coming back and when he answers *that* — well, it can go on forever. Inside, with the music on, the dog will quickly give up the idea of barking and settle in to listen to the music.

Another reason why dogs bark is because people generally allow them to pee across the road from where they live, or next door. You might think it's very innocent, but it's not. When your dog pees away from home base, its not just emptying its bladder, it's taking over new territory. You may keep a dog in a fenced yard and when you go out during the day you say, "This is your little patch, you've nothing to worry about." But the dog thinks differently. "No, I've got to worry about the street and next door, as well."

So anything that comes up and down the street, your dog thinks, "Well, I can't get out, so I'll have to shoo them away. I'll bark. And I'll bark louder until it's loud enough to drive those intruders out of my territory." It'll bark at other dogs, people, cars and anything else.

The solution lies in *not* allowing your dog to pee outside your gate or just down the street. If it means you have to take him for a little drive, so be it. If you're walking, every time your dog puts its nose to the ground, jerk upwards with the lead and that will quickly teach the dog that you don't want him scent marking. The message is, " If anyone's going to do that, it's going to be *me*, the leader." That will help the dog re-establish its borders. It will understand that he can only pee in his own territory.

Also, keep the dog in the back yard. Don't leave him out the front. If you do, you put him on sentry duty. Anyone coming to the house usually comes to the front door and the dog sees himself as the first line of defence. Even if the dog isn't an attacker, he'll bark to let you know there's someone coming.

Some people think leaving the dog out the front will let him see what's going on. But usually it excites him too much. Cars, people walking past, he naturally wants to engage with them. So when you do that you're telling him, "Rover, when I'm gone, you bark at anything that comes past." The poor old dog, thinking he's doing his job, keeps barking. He reckons he's going to get a reward when you come back. But what usually happens is he gets a flogging because all the neighbours complain that he's been barking.

Another major reason dogs bark is that they're bored. They've got too much energy and they don't get walked often enough. They try to organise their own exercise by barking and running laps around the yard. Some people think a yard is an exercise area. It's not, even if you put a tyre on a rope or something there. The dog needs to get out every day to explore and put something in its memory to think about during the hours it spends in the yard.

So please exercise your dog. Anyone will tell you a tired dog is a quiet dog. If I don't go out and walk my dogs two nights in a row, there's a racket going on out there. I can't resort to flogging dogs and things like that, because it's not right, eh? Walking does your heart good too. It gets the old blood going first thing in the morning before work.

Australian working breeds like kelpies, cattle dogs and dingo crosses, believe you me, need more exercise than anything. We're talking about twenty minutes of good exercise in the morning. That means running, chasing balls, something really workable that uses up a lot of energy. You also need a good forty-five minute to an hour's walk in the evening for sure, to compensate for the time it would have been working.

The dog would much rather come inside. That's a good pay-off for the rest of the exercise you didn't give it. They love being around you even more than exercise. So don't be sad if you can't give it that 100 kilometres a day. Give it a short walk in the morning, a big walk in the evening, then let it come inside to make up the difference. Being beside you in the house to a working dog seems as though they're still working because they love being close to you.

My dog is too noisy in the back yard

My dog Gus is out the back now, and he's barking like you wouldn't believe. I've been out there playing with him for the last twenty minutes or so, running about and jumping around. You would have thought that was enough, but obviously not. He's still barking like mad and still running around. I've even tried sending the kids out there to tire him out. They've been running around with the ball and everything but that seems to make him even more excited.

Gus obviously believes your back yard is a Bark Zone. It's a place he can bark to play, bark when the kids run around with each other, bark for food. He's now learning to bark to get you to come outside to tell him to shut up. He thinks he can bark anywhere. He just loves it because you've made him addicted to barking by playing with him.

From now on you have to make your back yard a Quiet Zone. All those games and stuff you used to do in the back yard will have to be transferred down to the park, because it doesn't matter how much he barks down there.

When the dog runs up to you in the back yard and wants to play, fold your arms way up high, lift your chin right up and absolutely ignore him. He'll learn to be calmer around you. As soon as he does, get him to do something for you — sit, lie down, or come to you. It doesn't matter what, as long as he's doing what you want. When he does, give him a little pat, yawn and look away and ignore him.

What you're trying to do is desensitise Gus from the act of playing and sensitise him to being calm, obedient and relaxed. If he's more persistent and he's barking when you're inside, he's wanting you to come out and bark with him. Get a couple of buckets of really cold water and keep them behind the door. If he keeps barking and running around, put him on a leash, then next time he barks walk out with one of the buckets, dump it over him and say, "Cold water."

Say nothing else. Don't interact with the dog. Just walk back into the house. If needs be, the second bucket is your backup. You might need two goes.

Gus will quickly learn that his barking doesn't bring you out to play. It brings you out to dump cold water on him. He'll quickly decide, "I'm not going to bark any more if that's what happens to me!"

My dog keeps barking at everything walking past our house

Our dog Peanut couldn't fight his way out of a paper bag, but whenever anything goes past our house, he's out there barking like hell, pretending to attack it. If something like another dog retaliates he's still out there barking, but heading the other way. I say, "Peanut, why are you putting us through all this stress? One day that dog's going to get you." I'm sure Peanut knows it too. My neighbours are getting really pissed off and I wouldn't blame them if they spoke to the council.

Peanut's been put out the front, right? He's been allowed to pee and extend his territory across the road. To him being put outside means only one thing. You've told him, "You're the sentry! If anything looks like a threat, you bark and we'll all come out and give you a hand."

You might not realise that the road's become part of your territory, but Peanut does. He's barking at everything so you'll come out and help him. When you come out and shout at him, he doesn't know why you're not doing it to the intruder who's passing by. There's a total state of confusion about exactly where the limits of the pack territory are. You think it ends at the fence. Peanut *knows* it's across the road.

Again, you've got to stop Peanut peeing across the road. He needs to be restricted to the back yard from now on. No room with a view out the front for him. Take the stress out of his life. That's what barking is, really. It's stress. "I'm afraid. Get away from my territory."

Leaving him out the back will help settle him down. If he keeps going across the road to make his scent mark, he's likely to be skittled. Keep him safe and you'll keep him unstressed and calm.

My dog howls when left alone

My big wolf-like dog, Scrapper, howls like a baby when he's left alone. It's quite embarrassing, never mind the noise for the neighbours. What's Scrapper trying to say to me?

Well, Scrapper could be exceedingly bored, or afraid. Believe it or not, big dogs get scared too. Or maybe he's confused about how you left him that morning. Maybe before you go out you go up to him and say, "Now Scrapper, I'm going out. I'll be back soon. I want you to be a good boy, okay?" Scrapper looks at you and sees you're all kind of upset. He can only think one thing. He things you're afraid. He thinks you're leaving the pack and you're leaving him there. He thinks you're never going to see him again.

With his little pea brain, Scrapper can't think beyond all that. That's where he's stuck all day, with that feeling that he's been abandoned. When you *do* come back by evening, he thinks it's by sheer luck. He thinks maybe you heard one of his howls at some stage and that's why you came back. That's also going to make him believe that the more he howls, the more likely you are to come back. When you do eventually come back, you're all excited and happy. There's giddiness all around him, which only reinforces the fact that you *did* go away but you *did* come back and you're all excited that he's still alive.

To fix this up, you're going to stop what I call "over-bonding" with your dog. You obviously spend too much time with the dog to compensate for when you're not there. That big "drop" when you're not there is confusing and mucking his head up a bit.

What you have to do is be nice and relaxed around your dog all the time. Don't spend too much attention on him. Act like you're a leader, that you're nice and relaxed and know what you're doing and where you're going.

Before you leave in the morning, do your level best to take your dog for a little walk. Just before you leave, give him a big juicy bone. When you produce the bone, it seems to him that his little walk amounted to a hunt. He didn't really see what was going on. Maybe he was looking the wrong way when the kill went down, but for you to come up with that bone, there was obviously a kill.

When you're leaving, just yawn, tilt your chin up high and wander off. None of that sooky stuff, "Oh I'll be back, don't bark." He won't understand that anyway. All he'll think is that you're worried and nervous. That's what's causing the howling.

I often tell people who have one dog that howls a lot because they're over-bonded, to get another dog. Shift that bond away from you. If you own a male dog get a female as his companion, and vice versa. Get a partner for the dog so it's not howling for you, it's got what it wants right there with it — another dog.

On top of everything else, that gives your dog something resembling consistency. The dog's life isn't all up and down all the time. One minute you're there, the next you're away for ten hours or so. Having a constant mate should take care of most of the howling.

If it isn't possible to get another dog, still do the unbonding things when you're around. And when you leave, put the dog in the laundry with some soothing music on the radio. Turn in up nice and loud.

What about the neighbours? Well, I'm sure they'd prefer to listen to some nice classical music than Scrapper's howling.

chapter 8

Liam's story

Leaders of the pack. Most people think my mate Liam has a disability but as far as being a good pack leader's concerned — he's positively gifted.

I got this call one day from a woman up the road. There was a problem with this dog called Goontzy. He'd had a colourful life. Goontzy had been left at her place by a former street kid, who'd been doing it tough — sleeping on the beaches and things like that. The dog was a pit bull terrier cross thing and it'd go anyone or anything that came near it.

The woman had three kids, including a young bloke aged about fourteen called Liam. She told me Liam had Down syndrome. I didn't even know what Down syndrome was until I went there and met him. The woman, Margaret, wondered if I could teach Liam to handle the dog.

When I first met them, I thought, "These people are crazy." What a great pair Liam and I made. There was me with my bloody Irish accent, talking at full throttle and there was Liam, who didn't seem to be able to speak at all. At first it just sounded like grunts to me.

I thought, "Hang on there. We can't understand each other. This is ridiculous. Slooooow down a bit." So that's what I did. At times I had to resort to sign language, but eventually I felt I was getting the message across to Liam about how to be a good leader. But really, I couldn't be sure.

We just had to go out with the dog and find out how much Liam understood. He seemed to get on with Goontzy all right. It's just that the dog wouldn't let anyone else near him.

Boy, did Liam open *my* eyes! He said nothing. He remained stony-faced. But as far as handling Goontzy, he didn't give an inch. Like any leader in the dog world, he let Goontzy know what he wanted by signals — simple moves of his head. If Goontzy didn't do what he wanted, Liam would just grab the lead tighter and make him lie down. After half an hour he had Goontzy just walking quietly behind him.

Liam was amazing. He was actually teaching *me*. The importance of using the right language was truly a revelation. Liam wasn't disadvantaged. He was over-advantaged. His lack of speech meant that he wasn't tempted to try to talk his way out of a situation like anyone else would have been.

In a friendly but firm way Liam showed this dog who was leader, saving it from the pound and certain death.

He made sure that whatever he wanted Goontzy to do, was done. He was recognising one of the dog's number one rules: "Don't tell me, show me." Goontzy was able to easily recognise a true leader who showed him very clearly what he wanted.

The point of Liam's story? Well, many so-called "ordinary" people seem to think that all this stuff I've been writing about is too complex, too demanding, for them. Bollocks! Anyone can do it.

We're talking about leadership, consideration and kindness. That's all a dog wants from humans. Demonstrate those things and any dog will do what you want. It's not submissiveness you'll create — it's loyalty. There's nothing better.

There's all sort of stuff spouted these days about cyberspace and how complicated the world has become. Forget it, man. Forget about cyberspace.

Get into dog space. It's simplicity itself.